ON THE ATTACK

ON THE ATTACK

The Batsman's Story

MATTHEW MAYNARD
WITH PAUL REES

MAINSTREAM
PUBLISHING

EDINBURGH AND LONDON

To my Mum, Sue, Tom, Ceri and the memory of my father

First published in Great Britain in 2001 by
MAINSTREAM PUBLISHING COMPANY (EDINBURGH) LTD
7 Albany Street
Edinburgh EH1 3UG

ISBN 1 84018 435 3

A catalogue record for this book is available from the British Library

Typeset in Courier and Giovanni
Printed and bound in Great Britain by Butler and Tanner Ltd, Frome and London

CONTENTS

THE GLAMORGAN SONG

Over the Severn and down to the Taff,
Like lambs to the slaughter they take on the Daff.
Now do they know how hard the Welsh will fight
As they trudge back to England, beaten out of sight.

We are Glamorgan, Dragons you and me,
Together we stand as the pride of Cymru.
We play to conquer and we play to thrill;
We play for the glory of the mighty Daffodil.

OWEN PARKIN

ACKNOWLEDGEMENTS

The authors thank the following for their help and support in the preparation of this book: Sue Maynard, Pat Maynard, Tom Maynard, Ceri Maynard; Mike Fatkin, Andrew Hignell, Duncan Fletcher, Dean Conway and the players and staff at Glamorgan CCC; Paul Russell of Andersen Consulting; Bill Clutterbuck; Menai Bridge Cricket Club, Bangor Cricket Club, St Fagan's Cricket Club; Margaret O'Reilly; Alan Edmunds and Bram Humphries of *Wales on Sunday*; Peter Pace of the *Daily Mirror*; Bernard Rees; Bill Campbell, Eddie Clark and Jessica Thompson at Mainstream Publishing; Huw John; David Llewellyn of *The Independent*.

FOREWORD

I have been fortunate to have been involved in first-class cricket since 1969, firstly as a player and more recently as a coach, and have experienced some successes – and a few failures! – along the way. As you might expect from modern sport, there have been a few disappointing times and some great moments. There have, however, been a handful of very special times for me. One was the County Championship-winning summer of 1997 as coach of Glamorgan.

During my career in cricket I have had the opportunity of playing with or being involved with an enormous number of cricketers. Some were ordinary, some were good, and there have been a small number whom I could only describe as outstanding. It is into this last category that I would place Matthew Maynard.

Here is a player who has a technique as good as anyone in world cricket today and has a range of shots that can dominate any bowling attack given even a sniff of an opportunity. Of those who were there or watching on television, who could forget the hundred he scored against Somerset at Taunton at the end of the 1997 season? It was the last match of the summer and Glamorgan had to win to take the honours. His hundred, made largely in the gathering gloom with five lights on the scoreboard, was one of the finest innings I have witnessed given the circumstances. And he didn't make a single until he was on 101!

That innings was something very special indeed. Not only was the occasion hugely important, but he made a very useful Somerset attack look ordinary. To put it further into context, Glamorgan had also had to defeat Essex in the previous match in Cardiff. Set 150 to win, they were 26 for 3 and it needed a steadying innings to see them home. Matthew provided it and led the side to victory. I would suggest that only the very finest of cricketers can play two such contrasting innings, with such high stakes, in successive visits to the crease.

It seems that England's loss has been Glamorgan's gain in that Matthew has never really been given a sufficiently long run to be able to prove his ability at the highest level. He has been labelled, as has happened with other players in the English game – in my view rashly in a number of cases – and it could be argued that one never truly loses that label. It is this stereotypical approach that can stifle natural talent and has resulted in England cricket losing out on exciting prospects. They are either the next Botham or Gower, or their heads are being called for, with little opportunity to develop and learn.

Matthew is not only a very talented batsman, he is also an outstanding fielder with great hands (although the number of finger breaks he has had suggest they are pretty brittle), has the ability to field anywhere – and having seen him keep wicket, I mean 'anywhere'! – and possesses the throw of a natural athlete.

To me, though, his most important attributes are his all-round cricketing knowledge, his sound man-management and the ability he has to lead from the front. These combine to make him a natural leader. Matthew has a unique feel for the game that is a rare commodity among captains, let alone cricketers. Some captains operate in a cautious, mechanical fashion and have a workmanlike relationship with the players in their teams. Matthew has that golden quality of being able to captain a side on gut reaction and cricketing nous.

Gut reaction must never be confused with lucky field placings or making bowling changes by rotation, for the sake of change. The instinct that Matthew displays is that of one of the shrewdest cricketing brains it has been my pleasure to encounter in cricket at any level. It is this quality that elevates a captain from the ordinary to the 'great'. To have a complete empathy with the job in hand, to know its requirements and demands without having consciously to think about it is one of Matthew's greatest qualities. His players respect him not through fear of his position but in the knowledge that he respects them and – although he can be hard when he needs to be – in the friendly relationship he develops with his team and the atmosphere that results. He is a natural captain.

I am sure Matthew Maynard will continue to entertain the cricketing public for the foreseeable future. I certainly enjoyed working with him; and the relationship that I built with him, both in cricket and, just as importantly, away from the game, is something I value very highly.

Duncan Fletcher
December 2000

1. FLETCH - MARK ONE

'You can't bat, you can't bowl and you can't field. You're all crap.'

It could have been a tabloid headline after another inglorious defeat inflicted on England, but the words were those of the national coach. We had lost a one-sided one-day international against West Indies at St Vincent in the winter of 1994, but the impact of the pacemen from the Caribbean was nothing compared to the reaction of our own Keith Fletcher.

It was my first, and only, England tour. It should have marked my arrival, at the age of 27, as an international cricketer, more than five years after I had made my début for England. I had had one Test at the end of the 1988 series against West Indies – the 23rd player to be used by the selectors that summer – before going back to Glamorgan with the reassuring words from the management ringing in my ears: 'We will be in touch'. I had been promised another chance. But the streets of the promised land are lined with telephones which never ring.

Given the whims of the England selectors then, you had to wrap yourself in the cocoon of your county. I was fortunate that Glamorgan had a good summer in 1993, pressing hard in the championship, winning the Sunday League and reaching the semi-final of the NatWest Trophy. We had a reasonably high profile as a county and our players were noticed: Steve Watkin and I were chosen for the tour of West Indies while Hugh Morris, Adrian Dale and Robert Croft went on the England A tour.

I played in the final two Tests of the series against Australia in 1993 and felt I had been chosen on merit rather than as a sop to the critics after another series had been lost. I had scored a century for Glamorgan against the Australians at Neath, an innings they had clearly digested because when I batted in the Tests they made adjustments to the field for me. I did not trouble them grievously. My final innings, at the Oval, was a good example of how adept Australia are at exerting pressure on opponents through their chirping. Shane Warne was bowling and I was coming down the wicket to him, looking to play the ball through mid-wicket. He remarked, 'If you don't get any runs this innings you won't be going on the West Indies tour.'

It had the desired effect. Suddenly you start thinking not just about the bowling, but about the future, and your footwork becomes less sure. Warne beat me a couple of times outside off stump with balls I felt I had to play in case they spun back. Finally, I let one pass and it took my off stump. As I walked past Warne, he made no comment. He did not have to: my stumps said it all.

Australia were chatty in the field, but not abusive. They were quick to exploit the insecurity of the England players, an uncertainty born of a selection system which gave too many players too few chances. The Aussies, in contrast, tended to stick with players once they had identified them as having the potential to succeed in international cricket. We had a revolving door; they had a combination lock.

As it turned out, that West Indies tour was the breaking, rather than the making, of me as an international player. I played in the first Test and the five one-day internationals, but after that I was a spare part, regarded as a frolic on the margin of the tour. When I returned home I took comfort in beer – washed up, washed out and bewildered after four months which should have been the making of me.

All sports are full of hard-luck stories, and as a Manchester City supporter I have witnessed more than my share of them, but I do not regard my career as a failure. I represented my country and I have been part of the most successful years in Glamorgan's history, but if I could change anything it would be that 1994 tour. It remains both the high and the low point of my career, the same door indicating arrival and exit.

Though I have probably reached the point where I will never play for England again in a five-day international (not that you ever abandon hope completely), I don't look back over my career with any sense of bitterness. I have played in four Test matches and I cannot complain that I was not given a chance. I would have liked an extended run in the side because I believe that I have the ability to succeed at the highest level, but looking back I can now appreciate that the England set-up in the days when I was capped was not one in which I was ever going to thrive.

My last Test for England was the first one in the West Indies in 1994. It was played at Jamaica, home of Courtenay Walsh and not the best ground for batting on. I had gone in during the final session of the first day and finished the evening unbeaten on 24, by which time I was the last of the recognised batsmen.

I had grafted for 90 minutes, but the next morning I felt I had to press on because we had lost a couple of wickets and I was with the tail. I had made 35 when Kenny Benjamin dug one in short and I looked to pull the ball to the square-leg boundary. It was not as short as I had thought and it hit me quite high on the pad: I was given out leg before. When I batted in the second innings Mike Atherton was at the other end: he warned me that the bounce had become unpredictable and I should look to play as often as possible at balls that were straight.

Winston Benjamin came in off a short run for my third ball and I knew from facing him in the County Championship that when he did that he was going to dig it in short. He did not disappoint and the ball brushed my glove and whistled passed my nose on its way to the wicket-keeper. What was to turn out to be my last Test innings ended up an inglorious duck.

Geoff Boycott had a chat with me at the end of the day's play and said that I had been stupid to give my wicket away in the first innings. 'If you had hung around and made 40 not out, you would have had an average of 40,' he said. 'Instead, your average is 17.5 and your place in the side for the second Test is in doubt.'

It did not make sense to me at the time, but it does now. What Boycott was saying was that I should have played for myself rather than the team, something which was not in my nature. Throughout my career, I have always taken more pleasure in how my side has done than in my individual performances.

One of my best moments with Glamorgan came in 1993 when we won the Sunday League against Kent at Canterbury. My contribution to the success was negligible: I scored a mere two runs, but I enjoyed the mother of all celebrations that night. On the other hand, when I won the man-of-the-match award in the Benson & Hedges Cup final in June 2000 after scoring a century against Gloucestershire, it was not even a consolation for coming second. I would happily have traded-in every run I scored for the victory. That is an easy thing to say, but I have never in my career felt good in defeat, success with the bat or not.

In my first spells with England, between 1988 and 1997, the emphasis was far more on the individual than the team and there was a selfishness within the dressing-room. When I turned up for my first cap, some players did not even acknowledge me, and my Glamorgan colleague Steve James suffered the same experience when he was called up by England in 1998: one player, who is in the current England squad, turned away when Steve said hello and did not utter a word to him for the entire five days.

I know from experience that that player's attitude has changed, as it had to when Duncan Fletcher took over as England coach at the end of 1999. Fletch is not one to let players take an ego ride. However it was my misfortune to be available for England at a time when it paid to be single-minded.

I remember when I was called up for my first cap against West Indies in 1988. It was the last Test of a series that had been another dismal one for England. The selectors were clearly acting more in hope than expectation and the county game was littered with one-cap wonders: the country which had exported cricket to the world was in meltdown.

On the eve of the West Indies Test the players attended a slap-up meal. The selectors were in attendance and someone from the then Test and County Cricket Board thundered on about how we were young men whom a nation was pinning its hopes on, how we were all in the side on merit and how he was sure that we would do very well. If he believed it, no one else did. For some of us it was to be the last, as well as the first, supper.

Boycott's point to me in the West Indies was that you had to look out for yourself because no one else would. England was 11 individuals rather than a team and with selectors often operating on a whim, averages mattered. You were not going to stay in the side because of what the team did – especially with England losing far more often than they won – but because you were not an obvious flop.

After my first Test in 1988, I joined the legion of players tried and discarded by England after just one chance. I was more fortunate than many, for I eventually got another opportunity. However I just wish that at the time, and again in the West Indies in 1994, I had challenged those in charge about why I'd been dropped, rather than meekly accepting it – not like Charlie Parker, who, after being constantly ignored in the 1920s, once grabbed hold of chairman of selectors Plum Warner's collar in a lift and threatened to hit him; but there is nothing worse than not knowing why you have been overlooked.

It got on top of me in the West Indies in 1994. I had played in the final two Tests against Australia in 1993, without particularly justifying my selection I admit, and I kept my place for the opening in Jamaica. There was a long gap between the first two Tests of that series because the five one-day internationals were then played all at once. I was chosen for all the one-dayers and again showed glimpses of what I could do rather than take an innings by its tail and turn it around.

I thought I would stay in the team for the second Test, but I had a clue that I might be on the way out the day before the side was announced. We were having a net and the first six batsmen worked out against the bowlers. The bowlers then put their pads on, with local cricketers sending them down deliveries. I had nothing to do until Keith Fletcher finally told me to have a bat. All the other players had gone in out of the heat: it was just me, Fletcher and the local bowlers.

Fletcher looked at me and said, 'Bring the balls in when you have finished.' And off he went. My net did not matter and neither did I for the rest of the tour. Whereas Fletcher up to that point had been supportive and eager to help, from then on I seemed to be nothing more to him than a slave: do this, do that without a please or thank you. I should have confronted him, but instead I said nothing and slowly tore myself up inside to the point where the following summer with Glamorgan I was little more than a barfly, looking at life through the bottom of a glass instead of working towards a fixed goal.

I hardly batted again on the tour. I had one chance before the fourth Test, but found myself down the order against a Board XI in Guyana. Mark Ramprakash had taken my place in the Test side, which left

Nasser Hussain and myself on the outside. Nasser was ahead of me in the order and, as the final session was drawing to its close, Fletcher asked him if he wanted a nightwatchman. Nasser said he did and I volunteered. I knew that if another nightwatchman went in, this would put me down to seven in the order and being down among the dead men was hardly going to do my chances of getting back in the Test side any good. But Fletcher turned his back on me and told my Glamorgan team-mate Steve Watkin to pad up and Watty ended up batting for the final few overs.

After close of play I ran back to the hotel, even though it was eight miles away: the loneliness of the long-distance runner. I knew it was the end of my tour. The road was full of potholes, cars with seemingly suicidal drivers kept narrowly missing me, and my head pounded. I was taking my anger and frustration out on my body rather than on Keith Fletcher. The team bus eventually passed me and Robin Smith joined me for the last few miles. I felt sick and had too many beers that night.

The following day, when I went in, I batted horribly and was out before Watty – cheaply. I was spent, emotionally. Fletcher was no longer acknowledging me and my self-esteem had gone along with my Test place. As an individual I am quite sensitive and, a long way from home, there was no one I could turn to. It was Mike Atherton's first tour as captain and he had enough to worry about with another series disappearing over the horizon. I should have been able to talk to Fletcher, but his attitude after our heavy one-day defeat ruled that out. He reacted in the way a supporter would do after too long in the sun and one can too many, kicking us when he should have been looking to pick us up. Instead of relieving pressure from players, he poured his own troubles onto them and our performances tended to reflect his demeanour.

I have won four England caps, I have played in 14 one-day internationals and I captained Glamorgan for five years, winning the championship and reaching our first one-day final for 23 years. When I reflect on my career in retirement there will be no regrets: I have achieved far more than I ever thought possible when I started my career as a nervous, raw teenager with Kent at the start of the 1980s.

I can see now that England players had to be selfish in the era of that 1994 West Indies tour. There was no real team identity because of the revolving-door selection policy. You had to look after yourself. My mistake was to think I had been selected for what I could bring to the side, whereas in actual fact, like others before and after me, I was there to silence the critics as the selectors reacted to defeats by bringing in players who had been scoring runs or taking wickets in the County Championship.

It was a hopeless policy and the championship was eventually blamed for England's international ills. It was first changed to a four-day format and then into two divisions, but I never felt that was addressing the root of the problem. When Australia were losing Tests in the 1980s, they looked at their domestic structure, but they eventually regained their status as the best team in the world by identifying players they felt would make it, and sticking with them. For us it remained a case of trial and error.

But how different it is under Duncan Fletcher. There was a scene when England were chasing victory against West Indies at Lord's in 2000 after bowling them out cheaply in the second innings. The tension was incredible as Dominic Cork and Darren Gough edged closer to the target. They went for a risky single, there was a mix-up and a run-out was on the cards. The television cameras panned to Duncan Fletcher – laughing. Whatever pressure he was feeling was not transmitted to the players.

I worked with Fletch at Glamorgan for two years, 1997 and 1999. Like me, he believed in the value of the team ethos and in our first year together we were criticised for dropping wicket-keeper Colin Metson in favour of Adrian Shaw. Metson was a talented player who in 1993 had been unfortunate not to go on an England tour. As a wicket-keeper, in technical terms, he was better than Shaw, no question about that. If it had come down to pure ability in 1997, Metson would have played. But Shaw had something that Metson had never had: a presence in the dressing-room which rubbed off on the other players, plus he offered more as a batsman.

Metson was not well liked by the other players and tended to keep himself to himself. I felt that, in a year when I believed we could win the championship having recruited Waqar Younis, the dressing-room had to be as one. Shaw was always quick with his congratulations or commiserations, someone who was clearly driven by the success of the team and whose part in our success that year was crucial in a way supporters will probably never be able to appreciate. I received a number of critical letters from supporters all through the season – even after we had won the championship, with one guy saying we would have wrapped it up sooner if I had picked Metson – and Adrian took some cruel abuse from a section of the crowd at Cardiff.

Some members of the Glamorgan committee also made their views known and from the outside it did look a strange decision. But the players understood it and Fletch backed me against the committee. Metto was in no doubt about why I had acted. I did feel pangs of guilt, though, because it was his Benefit year and, on the field, he had done a lot for Glamorgan.

If it hadn't been for the 1994 England tour, I'm not sure if I would have gone on to captain Glamorgan. I had been turned down for the position once, and committees and I do not go together, but the way I had been treated by Keith Fletcher and the awful summer I endured on my return home changed my mind. I started assuming responsibility, but ironically it was another Fletcher who was the making of the real me.

2. TOASTS

If I hadn't been a professional cricketer, I would probably have gone into the pub trade. My late father, Ken, worked for the brewers Greenall Whitley, first as a sales manager in Warrington and then as a publican in Menai Bridge.

I was born in Oldham in the year England won the soccer World Cup, a goal-kick away from Oldham Athletic's Boundary Park ground. My father was the biggest influence on my career. He did not suffer from pushy-old-man syndrome, preferring to offer advice when it was needed. He had been a professional sportsman himself, a bantamweight boxer who fought a final eliminator for the British title. He fought to support his family, but at the age of 27 had had enough. He was an imposing figure, standing at 6ft 2in. tall, and had a real presence about him.

I never harboured ambitions as a boy to play professional sport, even though I was not academic. I started to support Manchester City because my father used to bring signed memorabilia back with him from his travels. My elder brother, Charles, has always been a Manchester United supporter and I used to enjoy riling him: City were better than United when we were growing up, or so I liked to think.

I played a lot of soccer and rugby union as a teenager. I quite fancied myself as a rugby player, not bad as a full-back. I went to Ysgol David Hughes, which produced leading rugby players in Arthur Emyr and Iwan Jones, and at the age of 15 I played in a schools' trial match: North v South. I was high tackled and lost all feeling down one side. My neck was put in a collar and it took me six weeks to recover. That was the end of my rugby career.

I started playing cricket when I was 11, at school and for the Menai Bridge club. Dad promised to buy me a cricket bat if I scored a half-century. I hit 63 against Bangor Normal College and was presented with a Gray Nicholls scoop. I scored 147 with it in a school match against Amlwch and couldn't wait to get home and tell my parents about it.

I burst in full of excitement, reliving every shot. Dad nodded and said well done. It was only years later that I found out he had seen the whole innings. Not wanting me to know he was there, he had driven into the back car park and watched the match out of my sight. He made sure that I was never over-confident, but he never put any pressure on me. He taught me that sport was about entertainment and that you always had to be positive.

He played for a club side in Manchester, Ashton Nomads, a lower-order batsman who could hit the ball a long way and a left-arm chinaman bowler. He made me realise the importance of enjoying fielding. He used to say that a player would field in the course of a season for far longer than he would bat or bowl and that if you did not like that aspect of the game, you were wasting your time. To this day, I wince if I see someone yawning in the field.

Dad also stressed the importance of humour in sport and elsewhere. He used to call a girl from Llangefni I was seeing 'Rent-a-Ghost' because she was so pallid. When he saw a horse of that name was running in a race, he backed it at 10 to 1 and cleaned up. Meanwhile I was cleaned out, given the heave-ho after breaking my ankle playing soccer . . . Cricket has been my living, but it has also been great fun and has often had its humorous moments. It is small wonder that a number of former cricketers have become successful after-dinner speakers: their scripts write themselves.

The biggest regret I have in my career is not that I never scored a century for England or played more than four Tests but that my father never saw me play as a professional cricketer. He died of a heart attack in 1984 when he was 57. He knew I was going to get a contract with Glamorgan, but it had not been signed and sealed. When he took over the Liverpool Arms in Menai Bridge, after looking at a number of other pubs, he made a success of it but he lost his enthusiasm in his final few years. He became less concerned at the bottom line and after he died my mother, Pat, discovered a number of financial commitments which needed to be settled.

When I was in school I had never really thought what I would do for a career apart from taking over Dad's pub. I had had a trial with Lancashire at Old Trafford when I was 14, but I was too young and it did not work out. I played for Gwynedd Schools and then Wales Schools, doing better with the ball than the bat for the latter: I took six wickets against Ireland Schools at Buckley bowling in-swingers. I once bowled Tony Cottey, later to become a team-mate and vice-captain at Glamorgan, in a trial match. To this day he maintains that the ball hit a stone, but I know better.

By the time Dad died he had given up the Liverpool Arms. He had become a social host and had to take out a second mortgage which he did not endow. He was due to become a relief manager for the brewery, which gave him the advantage of remaining in the trade without being tied to a pub. My parents had bought their dream retirement house in Menai Bridge, a property which overlooked the Menai Straits.

Mum was forced to sell this house, to pay off Dad's debts, and had to start all over again in her 40s. She is a very strong character and it's from her that I think I have inherited my competitiveness and desire to win no matter what the odds. She bought a smaller house which needed renovating. Then, when I married my fiancée, Sue, and moved to Cardiff after joining Glamorgan, Mum came down with us and started working for a supply company for pubs – succeeding as I knew she would.

Unlike my brother Charlie, I was not academic at school. I left with a couple of GCEs and used to spend lessons looking out onto the sports field, though I never imagined I would be a professional sportsman. Mum used to urge me to work harder in school, but my reports were of the could-do-better, must-try-harder variety with teachers pointing out that my concentration tended to lapse (accusations later to be levelled at me as a batsman).

Charlie was heavily into music and I was persuaded to give it a go when I was 11. I played the cornet and some percussion in the Beaumaris Brass Band for three years and sang in the Bangor Cathedral Choir, but it was not really my scene. I was to music what Charlie was to cricket; but while he still turns out for a club side in Cardiff on occasions – the scruffiest cricketer you will ever clap eyes on – my musical career came to an abrupt stop. Charlie is now a peripatetic teacher who conducts orchestras and composes his own music.

While Charlie passed his A levels and went on to get a degree, I enrolled in the university of life. The making of me was three summers I spent with Kent from 1982, playing for their Second XI. Glamorgan had stopped playing in Colwyn Bay in those days and there was little contact between the two halves of Wales. I was playing in a match between a North Wales XI and a Chairman's XI at Bangor and scored a century.

John Bell, a hard-hitting batsman and leg-spin bowler, knew the Kent coach Colin Page and I was invited to a trial at Canterbury on 1 April 1982. I stayed in the Bat and Ball pub opposite the St Lawrence ground and was due to be met at the gates by Alan Ealham, a Kent stalwart. He was late and I wondered if I were the victim of some elaborate April fool. He eventually showed up and I played in a couple of trial matches, scoring 152 in the second. I was invited back for a six-week trial in the summer and made a few half-centuries without really proving myself.

I wasn't offered a contract, but Kent asked me to come back the following summer. It was the first time I had left home and I realised how sheltered I had been. In cricketing terms I was raw, but Colin Page made a big impression on me. He treated all the young players in the Kent Second XI as adults, impressing on us the importance of playing as a team and that if, for example, you went out one night and got roaring drunk, it would affect not just your performance the next day but the whole side's.

My cricket coach at school had been Phil Lewis, an enthusiastic and dedicated teacher of various sports. He stressed the enjoyment factor of sport and what drove him was his love of cricket, soccer and rugby, a devotion which rubbed off on a number of his charges. He let kids develop in their own time, but the worst thing he did was to get a coaching certificate because he then started to coach by the book.

As a kid, you want to bowl as fast as you can or hit every ball for six. You want to be the hero, the one everyone looks up to. It is a case of encouraging flair and responsibility at the same time, helping youngsters develop their skills. Too much of cricket, and other sports, today is about percentages and stifling the natural. Boys get categorised too early.

Colin Page established boundaries in which you operated. Over-indulge in a night to the extent that you were unable to take the field one day, and you were sacked on the spot. He didn't attempt to control what we did when we were away from the club – he merely reminded us not to let ourselves down – and he didn't see the world in black and white. There was one time when he *ordered* a player to get plastered.

Laurie Potter, a former captain of Young England, was desperate to play regular first-team cricket with Kent and he got himself so worked up that it showed every time he went out to bat. He was tense and weighed down with the pressure he had put on himself. Colin took him aside after one day's play, said he was fed up seeing him sitting around the hotel with a long face and told him to have a couple of beers too many.

Laurie batted the next day with a hangover but scored a half-century and never looked back after that. It was typical of Colin's man-management and I, like Laurie, desperately wanted to make it with Kent but I did not score enough runs in the three summers I spent there. The Second XI was strong, with players like Laurie, Graham Cowdrey, Steve Marsh, Steve Goldsmith, Simon Hinks, Rajesh Sharma and Stuart Waterton all contracted players. I found myself going in at number seven and it was difficult to get a bat, let alone make the centuries that I needed.

I told Colin in 1984 that I thought I was wasting my time. He made a telephone call to the Glamorgan coach, Alan Jones, and sorted out a trial for Glamorgan with me. But as I drove from Canterbury back to Wales there were tears in my eyes because, even though I was still only 18, I thought my chances of making it in professional cricket had gone and I drove like a maniac, lost in gloom.

It was also a wrench to be leaving Kent. When I first arrived there, I shared a flat with Kevin Masters, a useful seam bowler, his girl-friend Tracy and four-year-old son David. I learned more in my initial six-week stay with Kevin, known as 'Hoddy' because of his job as a builder, than I had done in all my years at school. He was a street lad, used to living off his wits, and he helped open my eyes. He quickly found out how incapable I was domestically. He had a gas stove and an electric kettle. One morning, he asked me to make a pot of tea, so I put the kettle on the gas ring and waited for it to whistle. It was not long before there was a horrible smell with fumes everywhere. Kevin had to wait a bit for his cuppa.

Having learned the art of making tea, I then progressed to toast. I knew I couldn't get that wrong because I'd made it often enough at home. I popped the bread under the grill and waited for it to brown, unaware of the toaster next to the cooker. On top of the stove was a hamster in a cage and I watched with increasing bemusement as he ran faster and faster in his little wheel, growing ever more frantic. I then smelled a familiar odour: the heat of the plastic was burning the bottom of the hamster's cage and I managed to rescue him just in time. I have improved since, but only to the extent that I can be trusted to stir a casserole.

Kevin's son was not impressed and I suspect he'd not forgotten the incident some 18 years later when we found ourselves on opposite sides in a NatWest Trophy match at Canterbury and he sent down some sharp out-swingers. It brought back to me visions of his hamster. It also made me realise that I was not young any more.

I had three enjoyable and character-forming summers with Hoddy. Kent paid on a match-to-match basis and it amounted to £120 a week, a good sum in those days, especially as accommodation was thrown in on top and the club had a generous expenses system. When I later signed for Glamorgan I was only on £2,000 a year. It was a different world in South Wales compared to the south-east. My future lay with Glamorgan, but Kent was where I had my grounding.

3. NUMBERS

Kent finished fifth in the 1984 championship, Glamorgan were thirteenth. Kent had been a major force in the British game in the 1970s, winning ten trophies – far more than any other side – while all Glamorgan had achieved in that decade was a trip to Lord's for the 1977 Gillette Cup final. I was going down in the world.

However it felt like up to me because this was my last chance to make it as a professional cricketer. I had a trial with Glamorgan and spent the rest of the summer playing for their Second XI. I found myself partnering the county's overseas professional Javed Miandad at Usk. Javed was having some batting practice after recovering from injury and he was the mainstay of the Glamorgan batting.

If Kent aimed to be the best, Glamorgan seemed happy to plod along. When it came to team spirit and getting fulfilment through enjoyment, there was no county like Glamorgan; but when it came to success, they struggled to win matches, let alone trophies. After winning the championship in 1969 and finishing runners-up the following year, Glamorgan had never finished in the top half of the championship and they were seen as a soft touch. They never had much problem in producing young talent, but their recruitment record was poor, both with players from other counties and from overseas.

Javed was an exception, but although his record for Glamorgan with the bat was outstanding, he could not drag an average side above the ordinary. Captain for only half a season in 1982, he could be disruptive. Nonetheless, for a young player like me starting out, he was someone to look up to and he had the attacking instincts which fired my game. I never really got to know him because he was fired by Glamorgan after not turning up for the start of the 1986 season. He'd just won the Calcutta Cup for Pakistan with a six off the final ball against India (which won him a car as well as the match) and become a national hero, fêted wherever he went. He decided to enjoy the attention rather than endure more strife with Glamorgan and by the time he got in touch with the county to say he would be a couple of months late, they told him to stay where he was.

Javed had an impact on my career because after the match in Usk, in which I scored a half-century, he told me to work on my technique against the short ball, pointing out that I needed to get over it more. That winter I spent weeks in the nets having short balls bowled at me until I reached the point where I had ironed out the weakness Javed had spotted. It was an early glimpse for me of the value of an overseas player, one which extends beyond what he does with the bat or the ball. But for Javed, I may never have made it as a professional cricketer.

I made a century in my second match for the Seconds and at the end of the 1984 season got offered a contract. It spared me the worry, for the time being, of wondering what to do with my two GCEs, but I knew that it was only a start. I had not arrived. The following year I played for the Seconds, scoring consistently without hitting a century. Our final game, ironically, was in Canterbury against Kent. We lost in two days, with Graham Cowdrey hitting 240. He had been dropped on 35 by Dai 'The Bounce' Williams, a quick bowler from North Wales who kept losing his contact lenses. Opponents must have thought we were doing ant impressions at times as we scrabbled on our hands in the field looking for one of Dai's lenses. He had them both in when Cowdrey lobbed up a dolly to him, but they may as well have been elsewhere.

At the end of the first day we retired to our hotel, which was by some way the dingiest I have ever stayed in. Alan Jones and the scorer, Gordon Lewis, were staying in a hotel next door – a far plusher affair with a bar – and we invited ourselves in. One of the players, Mike Cann, was sitting with a couple of Germans: as he was one of our not-out batsmen, Alan ordered him not to get drunk. Needless to say, Canny had a great night and on the first ball the next morning he had a horrible heave at a good delivery and was bowled middle stump.

Alan was not happy, especially when we capitulated so abjectly. It being the end of the season, he asked us after the match whether we wished to go home then or the following morning. Silly question. I went out with Laurie Potter and Kevin Masters and stayed the night with them. I returned to our hotel just before 9 a.m., only to find the coach about to leave. Fortunately, Ian Smith had rescued my kit from my room and I scrambled onto the bus. Alan Jones then said he had a message for me, Ian and Phil North. I wondered what we had done wrong, but he told us that we were to join the first-team squad in Swansea on the Friday for the championship game against Yorkshire.

To my surprise, I found myself playing. By Glamorgan's standards, it had not been a bad season: we were to finish twelfth with just four defeats, though unfortunately Yorkshire was one of them. Rain interrupted the match and I didn't find myself in the middle until the final day, when we needed 272 to win. I was batting at number five and came in at the healthy position of 120 for 3, but in those days Glamorgan had a remarkably consistent capacity to snatch defeat from the jaws of victory and we slid from 127 for 5 to 166 for 8. Soon Phil North, the last man, was at the wicket. I had not felt any first-night nerves and played my natural game.

David Bairstow, the Yorkshire cricketer who was so tragically to take his own life after he had retired, kept chirping from behind the stumps, 'This one only plays by numbers, he'll not last long.' When I got to 84, my highest score of the season, I knew that with no more wickets in hand I was not going to get my century by pushing the ball around. The field was set deep to offer me the single and get Phil on strike and with virtually every fielder on the boundary, fours were hard to come by.

Phil Carrick, an experienced left-arm spinner, was bowling and I decided to hit him over the top. I came down the wicket to his second ball and sent it over the sightscreen. It was premeditated. The next ball I did the same. I didn't hit it quite right and it only just cleared long on – I was hitting towards the pavilion, which is the slightly longer of the straight boundaries at St Helen's, but it was in championship terms relatively short.

St Helen's is not used much by Glamorgan now, because the county has bought Sophia Gardens in Cardiff, but it will always be steeped in our history. It was where Glamorgan used to host the major touring teams (Australia defeated in 1964 and 1968) and it was where Gary

Sobers achieved a world-record six sixes in an over in 1968 off Malcolm Nash. The ground, which is three-sided because of a rugby pitch, used to have an atmosphere all of its own, with the occupants of the old Mound Stand particularly vociferous. When I got to 96 with my second six, the volume increased.

Carrick was a wily bowler and I, a novice at 19, tried to read his mind. I decided that he would not expect me to come down the wicket a third time to him – so I did. The ball went a long way. I had become the youngest Glamorgan player to hit a century, and the first to do so on début since Frank Pinch in 1921, the county's first year in the championship. After I'd reached the landmark, I should have turned to Bairstow and, in reference to his numbers gibe, said, 'Two, three and four that over', but I do not speak much when I am batting and, anyway, the best lines usually come to you after the event.

Triumph and failure came together that over. I played the fifth ball out into the covers and should have taken the single that I had been offered with the field still back, but I'd not properly refocused after the applause for the century. I tried to cut the last ball, but guided it into the hands of backward point. We had lost by 35 runs.

I walked off to a standing ovation and champagne corks were soon popping. It was a strange feeling: everyone was cheering but we had lost a match. It took a while for what I had achieved to sink in and much was made of my hitting three consecutive sixes to reach the three-figure mark. I had hit five sixes in all and 13 fours in a 98-ball innings and what was important to me was that, despite the fact it was my first championship knock, I had played my natural game. I just wish Dad had been there to see it.

Geoff Boycott came into our dressing-room and came up to me, ignoring everyone else, and shook my hand. 'Well played, lad,' he said and walked off. It was a simple gesture, something he did not have to do, and it meant a lot to me. As batsmen, Boycott and I were opposites, but I have always got on very well with him.

When at the crease, he didn't always conform to his stereotype as a player who never took any risks. The day before my maiden century, we had played Yorkshire in a Sunday League game at Swansea. Boycott was their most attacking batsman, revealing a full array of shots, and we were delighted when he was out in a freak dismissal: Jim Love hit the ball back firmly and it was deflected on to the stumps with Boycs out of his crease. It is fair to say that he was not pleased.

I made eight in our innings during that match at Swansea, perishing in the cause because rain had reduced the number of overs each side was allowed. Yorkshire needed four to win off the last ball: they had been in control when Boycott was at the wicket, but Geoff Holmes took five wickets with his seamers to swing the match our way. I was fielding on the mid-wicket boundary when the final ball was hit along the ground my way. St Helen's can be a treacherous ground for fielding if you are on the part of the outfield which doubles up as rugby turf, but there was no divot to make a fool of me that time and we sneaked home.

I stayed in the side for the final three championship matches and should have made a century in my next innings, against Nottinghamshire at Trent Bridge. I was batting with Glamorgan's South African skipper Rodney Ontong in our first innings and was on 58 when I got yorked by Andy Pick, one ball away from the tea break – an in-swinger I can still see now. Rodney went on to make 130 and took 13 wickets in the match, which we won.

He was to give up the captaincy three months into the 1986 season, frustrated to the point of despair that we were going nowhere as a side, throwing away promising positions time and again, unable to press home an advantage. I was Rodney's driver in 1986 and he would get so upset at the end of matches that he'd hit his head on the window of the dashboard. If we did win a game, it tended to be because of a superb individual performance rather than because we had performed as a team. After Rodney had decided that he didn't want to go on any more, Hugh Morris became our seventh captain in five years and, at the age of 22, the youngest ever.

Three years later Hugh also gave up the captaincy halfway through the campaign, and there were four seasons in the 1980s when we were led by two different captains. Rodney's final game in charge was against Northamptonshire: it ended in a draw, but we had the worst of it with Rob Bailey hitting a double-century. As so often happens, a new broom enjoys a clean sweep and we won our first match under Hugh, but there was no disguising the fact that we were lacking as a team – in terms not so much of ability, but of attitude. We were not winners.

I was sorry that Rodney resigned because he was the type of captain we needed, a hard man who was close during his career to being chosen for England (having qualified on residence). He left me out of the side at the start of the 1986 season, even though I had made my mark the previous August, and when I was brought in to face Middlesex at Lord's, I batted at number seven and came in at 25 for 5. The West Indian Wayne Daniel was bowling at his fastest on an unpredictable wicket and I joined Rodney at the wicket.

Daniel bowled me a bouncer and I stared him out. It was the end of the over and Rodney marched down with a thunderous look in his eyes. 'Look at your bootlaces the next time, boy,' he barked. I tried to explain that it was psychology on my part and that I was trying to wind him up and make him lose his line. Rodney snorted and walked away as if I were a delusional half-wit.

The first ball of Daniel's next over was short and wide, which Rodney sent on its way to the boundary. No word of thanks to me! I ended up top scoring with 57 before being dismissed by Mike Gatting: what was worse, I hit my own wicket. I played the following match against Somerset, made two low scores and was dropped again. I was quickly reinstated after a heavy defeat by Essex and made 129 against Warwickshire at Edgbaston. I remained in the side and was to suffer the ignominy of being dumped into the Second XI only one other time, by Alan Butcher in 1989. (I also played for the Second XI in 1994, when the first team had a week off, after a wretched start to the season.) By then, Glamorgan had, at long last, turned the corner.

4. THE KING AND I

I have never had any regrets about joining Glamorgan, but we certainly were a soft touch in my early years. We had some good players, but we did not know how to win matches. As a social club there was none better than Glamorgan, but we lacked an inner hardness and while other sides were collecting trophies, we kept changing captains.

Three men were to make a crucial difference. Tony Lewis, the former Glamorgan and England captain, became the club's chairman. Alan Butcher, an opening batsman who was a member of England's one-cap club, joined from Surrey. And, in 1990, Viv Richards became our overseas player: the King took over the Principality.

Part of Glamorgan's problem had been its large committee, an unwieldy body of well-meaning amateurs which interfered too often with what happened on the field. Tony Lewis, who had achieved fame after his retirement as a player by anchoring BBC TV's Test match coverage, was effective as a chairman because of his experience as a first-class cricketer. He had captained Glamorgan to the 1969 championship title, the last time the county had won anything, and he was shocked at how markedly things had declined since then.

Alan Butcher joined in 1987. We had finished bottom of the championship the previous year and, at first, I wondered why we had signed Butch. Glamorgan had in recent years signed former England internationals who were coming to the end of their playing days, only to find that these players lacked motivation and were also totally unprepared for the relatively amateur way in which the club was run. However, Butch was different. He still had a lot to offer as a batsman, but he did not come to Glamorgan to earn some easy money. He ruffled a few feathers and some players didn't like him – generally the ones he had identified as not pulling their weight. He was a hard man, motivated by winning, and there was no way he was going to put up with what had gone on before: within two years he had taken over from Hugh Morris as captain and Glamorgan's rise started at that moment.

Both Tony and Alan recognised that something seismic had to happen if attitudes were going to change. We had finished bottom in the championship again in 1989, despite Butch leading the way with 1,632 runs: only three of us passed the 1,000 mark and I only made it at the end of the season, having completely lost my form after a promising start. We had propped the table up for three seasons out of four, winning nine matches and losing 30 during that sequence. Never before had we won the wooden spoon in successive seasons.

Tony somehow persuaded Viv Richards to join us. Viv was nearer the end of his career than the beginning, but he was by some way the most famous cricketer in the world, a man of huge presence who had helped himself to more than his share of runs against Glamorgan in the past. One look from Viv could cow a bowler into submission. The word 'legend' has become a cliché in sport, but Viv was a legend among legends and the fact that Glamorgan had signed him on a three-year contract was concrete proof of the club's renewed ambition.

Viv did not disappoint. He was still captain of West Indies, then the undisputed world champions, but he identified with the underdog. I think the challenge of helping a county as unsuccessful as Glamorgan to win something appealed to him, but he never threw his weight about in the dressing-room or played the big 'I am'. He quickly became one of the players, with one difference: when Viv spoke, everyone listened.

His first game for us was at Warwickshire in the Benson & Hedges Cup. He failed with the bat, but in typical Viv fashion won the game for us with the ball – the final ball of the match. We had made 196 for 9 and Warwickshire were 193 for 7 when Viv came in off his lazy, uncoiling run. Facing him was Dermot Reeve, the master of the improvised shot in one-day cricket. Viv had already taken two wickets and his last delivery hit Reeve on the pads before going down the leg side to the boundary rope. Warwickshire thought they had won, only for Viv to appeal for leg before. It looked dubious to me, but Viv had a way about him. Up went the finger: the legend lived on.

Viv had taken the field with the type of sweater worn only by players the county had capped. The custom, when it came to overseas players and internationals signed from other counties, was to cap them immediately but make the formal presentation after they had hit some runs or taken a haul of wickets at a match in front of the Glamorgan crowd. With a player of Viv's stature, the fact that he was at the county was enough and Butch had had no hesitation in giving him the sweater before he had played a match – quite rightly. During the Warwickshire game, however, a member of the committee approached Butch and asked what Viv was doing wearing the sweater of a capped player. Butch glared at him for asking such a stupid question.

As soon as the news of Viv's signing had come out, Glamorgan were swamped with membership requests and we achieved national publicity out of all proportion to our position. As I was to find when I took over as the Glamorgan captain, too many on the committee think in micro, rather than macro, terms. They are obsessed by trivia and archaic traditions. Butch, an Englishman, was doing everything he could to get a laughing stock to be taken seriously and someone who should have known better took issue with him over nothing. When Butch told the story to me, he was shaking his head in disbelief. Viv was to score a century on his championship début for us, but one of the chores of being a county captain is the drip-drip effect of minor interference: after five seasons from 1996, I personally couldn't take any more.

Butch had the strength of character to treat fools with the contempt they deserved and not worry about the consequences. His predecessor, Hugh Morris, was a more sensitive person who had taken over the leadership before he was ready for it and who became so worn down by the demands of the job off the field that he felt the captaincy was affecting his form. Hugh and Butch were opening partners, two left-handed batsmen with a greed for runs. We finished eighth in 1990, our highest position in the championship for 20 years, with Butch and Hugh both scoring more than 2,000 runs. Between them, they passed the 50-mark 41 times in 42 matches and they put on a dozen century stands.

Amazingly, considering the success of the partnership, they did not speak to each other off the field, just like Andy Cole and Teddy Sheringham at Manchester United. It wasn't only that they were totally contrasting personalities: the fact that Butch had taken over as captain from Hugh during the 1989 season had created tension, though neither of them would speak about it. I think Hugh felt that Butch had been brought to Glamorgan with the promise that he would soon take over the leadership. Something was said and Hugh was someone who held things against people – one of the reasons why I felt that, in terms of temperament, he was not the ideal captain. Whatever the reason for their mutual silence, and it was bizarre given the dressing-room spirit we had fostered, the pair were professional enough to put aside their differences on the field in what was a summer for the batsmen. I passed 1,500 runs and Tony Cottey scored 1,001; but topping the averages was Viv, whose 1,425 runs included seven centuries.

Hugh was not my type of captain, too regimented and inflexible even if his attention to detail and planning were meticulous, but there was no questioning his value as a player. He was a tough and courageous opening batsmen who got harshly treated by England. He was the mainstay of our batting for years, regularly scoring runs at crucial times. He left a massive hole when he retired after the 1997 season to take up a post with the England and Wales Cricket Board. There was still a lot more to come from him.

Despite his average of 61.95, the difference that Viv made was as much in our minds as it was in his deeds. That July, we played Sussex in Cardiff in the NatWest Trophy. We were put into bat and made 283 for 5 in our 60 overs, Viv top scoring with an unbeaten 74. Sussex were cruising at 229 for 2 with ten overs to go. Paul Parker and Alan Wells were both approaching their centuries and the game was all but over. As the crowd started to drift away, so did the attention of some of our fielders, before a booming voice from the outfield woke everyone up.

'Get your hands out of your pockets, boy,' Viv bellowed at Ian Smith and the match turned in that moment. Viv had been leading by example in the field: not even Parker, one of the best runners between the wickets in the game, dared take two to deep cover where Viv was prowling menacingly. Even in his late 30s, he moved with agility and he invariably threw the ball directly into the wicket-keeper's hands, hard and flat.

It became a different game. Nigel Cowley took two wickets in an over, Viv bowled Parker and eight wickets fell in the space of seven overs to leave us winners by 34 runs. It summed up what Viv Richards brought to Glamorgan. He detested losing, and whereas most of us, subconsciously at least, had accepted Sussex were going to win – waiting for something to happen rather than making it happen – he was not prepared to concede anything. Gradually we lost our softness and when we won the county championship in 1997, we owed a debt of gratitude to Viv because he had helped put back the belief into Glamorgan cricket.

He vowed to help Glamorgan win a trophy and was true to his word. He was at the wicket with Tony Cottey when we defeated Kent at Canterbury to win the 1993 Sunday League, our first one-day trophy. The way Viv celebrated afterwards, sipping on brandy and coke and puffing on a fat cigar, it was as if he had never won anything before, and the pleasure he derived from helping an unfashionable county succeed was without any question genuine.

One moment from that weekend summed up Viv. The Sunday League match was sandwiched in between our championship match against Kent which had been due to start on the Thursday only for rain to wash out the first day's play. They won the toss and batted on the Friday. Thrashing our bowlers to all parts of the ground, they went on to make 524 for 6 with their West Indian all-rounder Carl Hooper hitting a double-century.

We were then rolled out for 144. I had been unable to bat because of a neck injury and we expected Kent to enforce the follow on. But they chose to bat again, looking for some practice ahead of the following day's Sunday League match, and ended up setting us an unlikely target of 476. We ended up 7 for 2 on the Saturday night and were feeling very down in the dressing-room. Viv was still walking with a swagger and strolled out onto the balcony. We thought he was taking in some fresh air, but the Kent balcony was next to ours and he called over Hooper for a word.

The conversation could be heard in both dressing-rooms. 'Hoops, man,' said Viv. 'You tell your captain that if he's going to f*** with the game, the game will f*** with him.' He was angry that Kent had not made us follow on, feeling there was no good cricketing reason for the decision. Kent's captain, Steve Marsh, would not have needed Hooper to relay the message: he would have heard it all too plainly himself.

The Sunday League match was finely poised when Viv came out to bat. We had restricted Kent to 200 for 9 in their 50 overs and 67 from Hugh Morris helped us to 141 for 4 when Tony Cottey joined Viv at the wicket. They were our last two recognised batsmen and we needed them to stay together. Viv had entered to a standing ovation and he was on 14 when the game's defining moment occurred. Duncan Spencer, who had trapped me leg before for two, dug one in short and Viv went to pull the ball to the square-leg boundary.

He was late on the shot and the ball went straight in the air to Spencer, who then did a victory dance. All the Kent players came up to congratulate him, including wicket-keeper Marsh. Viv stood where he was, leaning casually on his bat: only he had seen the outstretched arm of umpire David Constant signalling no-ball. As Marsh walked unhappily back past the stumps to his mark, Viv had a few words for him. 'I told you, man. If you f*** with the game, the game will f*** with you.' Cotts and Viv, who finished with 46, took us home to joy unconfined.

We finished the championship match on the Monday after the mother of all parties, only getting halfway to our target. It was Viv's final knock in first-class cricket and we had introduced a fines kitty for any batsmen who blocked three balls in a row. Viv was amazing, carving the bowling everywhere, and it looked certain that he would go out with a century until Hooper had him caught for a brilliant 83 which summed up the man.

Viv fitted easily into the dressing-room. There were times when he liked to be alone, but he was always approachable, always willing to give advice to the younger players. Only once can I recall any problems with him. It was in the summer of 1992 and I had taken over as captain from Alan Butcher, whose season, and subsequently his career, was cut short by a knee injury.

We were playing Essex at Chelmsford and before the match we had a net. Our net was congested and Robert Croft spotted that Essex only had two players in theirs. He went over and joined in, bowling a couple of deliveries a minute rather than one every three minutes as he was doing in our net.

When we went into the dressing-room afterwards, Viv tore into Crofty and it followed a disruptive pattern at that time. Butch would have been able to deal with it, but as acting captain, I didn't feel I had the proper authority and so raised the matter with David Morgan, the club chairman. I wanted Viv to miss the next couple of matches because he had started to affect morale.

David had a word with Viv and discovered that he had some personal problems. He was given a couple of weeks off and when he returned he was his old self. Overseas players do tend to throw one wobbly a season. We signed the Australian opening batsman Matthew Elliott for the 2000 season and he fitted into the dressing-room superbly even though we had been warned that he had a reputation for being slightly awkward.

We were playing in Northampton when someone spilled a glass of orange juice over the box containing Matt's kit. I was away on England duty, but the guys told me that he went ballistic and really lost it, ranting and raving before locking himself in the toilet. He was going out to bat after tea and threw his wicket away with a reckless shot in anger. I spoke to him afterwards and he said that he had just lost it.

You have to make allowances because players coming from abroad have to settle into a new way of life and there are bound to be stresses and strains. All you ask of them on the field is that they turn in a couple of match-winning performances for you. Viv and Matt did that, hitting centuries when they were needed.

Viv's finest hour for us came at Southampton in 1990. Hampshire had set us 364 off a minimum 102 overs and we had never made that number of runs in a fourth innings to win a match. It looked all over for us at 139 for 5, but where there was Viv Richards there was hope. We needed 12 off the last over, bowled by Viv's West Indies colleague Malcolm Marshall, probably the best fast bowler of his generation. Marshall against Richards had been a contest within a contest and no one who was at the ground that day could deny the value of overseas players in our game.

Viv was the winner this time, unbeaten on 164, Marshall's final three balls going for four, six and four. We had successfully chased a target in excess of 300 in our previous match, Viv and I scoring centuries at Northampton, and to bat with him was an education. He intimidated opponents by the way he walked to the wicket, in a cap rather than a helmet, usually with gum in his mouth and a dismissive look on his face.

It was because of Butch and Viv that I developed my ambition to captain Glamorgan. They were both good readers of the game, but what made an impression on me was the way they would not allow things to drift. They believed in the value of the unexpected: Butch opened the bowling one match and I shared his view that leadership involves risk and making instant decisions. They may both be long gone from Glamorgan, but their legacy lives on.

5. THE DOME

County cricket has been ridiculed in recent years for having a softness which has held back England at international level: too many clubs with a surfeit of players on their books have been blamed for a decline in standards by many in the game. It is not a view I share. County cricket is far more professional than when I started. The twin problems have been England's knee-jerk selection policy, which David Lloyd and his successor as national coach Duncan Fletcher have done a lot to alleviate; and dreadful wickets which encourage medium-pace trundlers rather than batsmen and spinners.

The gap between first- and second-XI cricket is enormous, so much so that the more time players spend in the reserves, the less prepared they are for the county game. That was something of which I was conscious during my five years as Glamorgan captain and there is an argument for counties to have fewer contracted players, using second-XI matches to look at promising club players and emerging youngsters.

When I was growing up my cricketing heroes were David Gower and Ian Botham. There was an elegance about Gower's batting which made it look effortlessly easy for him. He always seemed to have time, never ruffled or breaking out in a sweat, the epitome of English calm. He had an air about him which suggested he didn't care less. He was dismissed once playing for Hampshire against us with his usual casual disdain, pulling a short ball from our quick bowler Daren Foster to square leg. Daren gave it everything when it came to his celebrations, as if he had just won an Ashes series for England; Gower just shook his head, gave his familiar lop-sided grin and walked off.

I have been compared to Gower, which is flattering, but I am not as pleasing on the eye as he was. One thing we had in common is that we were both turned down by Kent, the county where he was educated. He was not a percentage player, and neither am I, but there was nothing like Gower in full flow. Botham was a totally different character, all muscle and sinew, menacing and imposing: Bully Beef.

The first time I faced his bowling was in 1987 when Glamorgan were playing Worcestershire at New Road. I had never enjoyed watching cricket as a boy, preferring to be out playing, but I was glued to the television in 1981 when Botham took on the Australians at Old Trafford and Headingley. There was something about him: he would get wickets with bad balls or survive an outrageous shot. Like Viv, he had a presence, a strong personality which helped him make things happen – one of the greatest cricketers in the history of the game.

When I faced him at New Road I was feeling pleased with myself. I'd been awarded my county cap at Weston-super-Mare two weeks before, having scored 160 against Somerset. Botham's first ball to me was a bouncer which whistled past my face. Beefy's follow-through took him all the way to my crease where he looked at me and snarled, 'Welcome to the Pleasure Dome.' I became a bag of nerves and Botham, realising he had scored a direct hit, ran in faster. I played and missed at a couple of his out-swingers and received more advice about my technique.

After two overs of my making a fool of myself Botham told me, in Anglo-Saxon terms, that a bat was for using. I expected the next delivery to be short, and it was. The words of Javed at Usk came back to me and I quickly got into position, hooking it one bounce for four. He kept on bowling short and I kept on attacking him. He then came off and for me it was an important battle won: if you are intimidated, your ability counts for nothing and the experience hardened me up. So much for county cricket being soft.

Sledging, or 'chirping' as I prefer to call it, has long been part of the game, but most of it is aimed indirectly at a batsman in an attempt to unsettle him. When I made my début for England against West Indies in 1988, Viv Richards was leading the side from his usual position in the slips. He had yet to join Glamorgan and I really knew him only by reputation. As I was taking guard he piped up, 'Come on guys: let's have some chin music. See if the man's head can dance around.' I knew

I was not about to be treated to a succeession of juicy half-volleys. Viv was looking at his bowler, but speaking to me, and the message was heard loud and clear.

I have never answered a bowler back in my career – partly because it is not in my nature and partly because by the time I think of a suitable response the moment has gone. The Glamorgan opener Steve James is different and will always have a pop back and I was impressed with two of Glamorgan's young players in the summer of 2000 when Nottinghamshire's fast bowler Paul Franks tried to intimidate them. Ian Thomas, who had broken into the side after starting the season playing club cricket, hit Franks to the boundary after receiving a volley of invective and gave him some choice Anglo-Saxon language in return, to the effect of 'fetch that'. Franks may have been an England hopeful and Thomas a newcomer to the county game, but Ian was not going to be intimidated.

Mark Wallace, our England Under-19 wicket-keeper, went one better. Franks treated Mark to a few choice words before the 18-year-old replied with remarkable coolness, 'There are ten blokes in our dressing-room who cannot stand you. Stop being a prat or you will make it eleven.' It shut Franks up totally. The confidence of youth!

The 1987 season was a successful one for me. I topped Glamorgan's batting averages with 1,626 runs at an average of 40.65. I reached 50 on 14 occasions, but only went on to make two centuries. I established a number of landmarks: my century before lunch against Somerset at Weston was the first time a player had achieved the feat for the club since Javed seven years before; I had the fastest ever half-century for Glamorgan, taking 14 minutes and 22 balls to reach the landmark against Yorkshire at Cardiff (it's not worth mentioning the fact that it was against declaration bowling); I hit 30 off one over that day, a post-war best by a Glamorgan batsman; my 30 boundary sixes that season were more than anyone else in the championship; I equalled Jim Presdee's record of the youngest Glamorgan player to be capped; I took the highest number of catches by a fielder in the championship, 30; I won the *Cricketer*/Beefeater Gin Spirit of Achievement Award for 1987; and when I hit 50 off 33 balls in the Sunday League match against Somerset at Weston, it was the fastest televised half-century of the summer.

I had started the season coming in at number six or seven, but by the end was at number four, the position where I have batted constantly almost ever since. I was being mentioned as a potential England international, but I was delighted to be offered a new contract by Glamorgan. As it was my first full summer in the side, it was always going to be an important campaign for me. Teams on the circuit had got to know my style and temperament and I was aware that they would be devising ways of getting me out, so to play consistently well was essential if I were to make it as a first-class cricketer.

I had reached 1,000 runs at the end of the 1986 season – just – having played seven matches for the reserves and I was to be dropped only once more in my career, in 1989 by Alan Butcher after a depressing run of low scores. I got to the 1,000 mark against Worcestershire at New Road in our last-but-one match of the campaign, Rodney Ontong delaying his declaration until I made the four-figure mark: Graeme Hick reached his 2,000 runs for the season in the same match, scoring a century as they reached their target of 302 with ease.

In those days a batsman was judged to be a success if he reached 1,000 runs in a season. There were 24 championship matches in a campaign then, compared to 16 now, and you did not have to have a prolific season to achieve the feat. Today batsmen prove their worth not so much by reaching 1,000 runs but by playing match-winning innings: it is possible to score only 700 or 800 runs in a season but still prove your worth in the side. When Surrey won the championship in 2000, they did so without any of their batsmen making it to 1,000. It is virtually impossible now to score 2,000 runs in a summer. Getting to 1,500 is a notable achievement, another reason why comparisons between today and yesteryear are often pointless.

One interesting statistic from the 1986 season is my one-day average: it barely made it into double figures, ironic considering that I have often been described in recent years as a one-day specialist. That's a tag which annoys me, not least because I have a first-class average which is as good as many of the batsmen in the England squad – and I am approaching 50 centuries, having been dismissed in the 90s on some 20 occasions. It is a misconception based on my aggressive style of batting which is seen, wrongly, as a feature more of limited overs cricket than of the four-day game.

I have scored three double-centuries, but the one-day label does get to me and I do now have a problem when I get into the 90s, putting pressure on myself when before I did not give it a second thought. In the 2000 season I was on 97 against Essex in Cardiff when the spinner Paul Grayson lobbed one up to me. There was a gap through mid-off and I went for the shot which would take me to my century. Unfortunately, the ball hit the non-striker Adrian Shaw, whose bat flew out of his hand. I took a single off the final ball of the over before clipping a half-volley straight to the hands of mid-wicket two short of my century.

I am a fatalist, believing that things happen for a reason: if something happens on a cricket field, it is meant to be. I was still angry to be out for 98 – though if someone had said when I went out to bat that I would score that many I would have taken it – but when I look at the scoreboard now it is for the team's score more than my own. I have still got a long way to go to catch up Alan Jones, the former Glamorgan opener, who was stranded in the 90s on 40 occasions in his career.

Batting in one-day cricket is a totally different discipline to championship cricket, more about working the ball around the field and keeping the scoreboard moving with fields set deep after the first 15 overs. There is more scope to hit out in the four-day game because the boundaries in front of the bat are often left unguarded. It was difficult to adjust to the two very different forms of cricket when I broke into the Glamorgan side and I concentrated on the championship.

It can be dangerous and counter-productive to expect young players to adapt immediately to both the one- and four-day games. After the Glamorgan slow left-arm bowler Dean Cosker had gone on an England A tour at the end of the 1990s, he came back a shadow of the bowler he had been at the end of the previous season. The loop he had in his bowling had gone and his deliveries were flatter and quicker.

It took us two years to get him back to where he had been and in that time I did not play him much in one-day cricket, preferring to encourage his flight in championship matches, and there were signs in 2000 that his career was about to take off again. I do not know what it is about England A tours – whether young players who go on them feel they have arrived before they have achieved anything, or whether the coaching owes more to indoctrination than advice. Players sometimes come back with inflated opinions of themselves and very often are less effective cricketers than when they left. At Glamorgan, we have suffered from off-spinner Robert Croft's various stints with England: another bowler who had a well-flighted stock ball, his bowling became progressively flatter until he was bowling at virtually the same speed as a medium-pacer.

He was dropped by England on more than one occasion but, unlike me, he asked for reasons why he had been left out and made the selectors and coach accountable. The advice he got was mixed and he became obsessive about what he had to do to get back into the side.

Once at Trent Bridge, in a televised one-day match, I wondered why he kept looking over at me in the field after he had bowled, as if seeking reassurance. It was only after a few overs that I realised he was watching the moving camera which was recording the speed he was bowling at. When he got below 50 mph he let out a huge roar as if he had just taken the crucial wicket. He had adopted new tricks in the previous couple of seasons, such as varying his approach and bowling from two yards further back, after being criticised for being a containing rather than an attacking spinner. He was desperate to prove himself with England and became guilty of trying too hard. His natural style, the one which had got him capped in the first place, had long gone and he was trying to become the bowler he thought the selectors wanted him to be rather than the one he was.

He lost his way, like many England batsmen and bowlers of his generation. Back in 1986, Rodney Ontong told me to be myself and to trust my judgement, advice I have followed throughout my career. There are times when you pay for not playing percentage cricket, but if you are not true to yourself, no one else will be. David Gower and Ian Botham were my inspiration – the curators of the Pleasure Dome.

6. MEDIUM OR RARE?

I went from the bottom to the top and back again in 1988. Glamorgan once again picked up the wooden spoon in the championship, marooned by 39 points at the bottom after winning just one match, against Warwickshire at Edgbaston at the end of the season. (And we did our best to lose that: they were chasing 193 and were 107 for 9 when Norman Gifford joined Gladstone Small – not the ideal pair of batsmen on a wicket which was offering considerable assistance to the bowlers, but they came within a boundary of establishing a world record last-wicket winning partnership before our fast bowler Greg Thomas removed Small and we won by four runs.)

I topped our batting averages after scoring 1,439 runs. Again, though, I did not convert enough fifties into centuries, with a 3–11 split. However it was good enough to earn me a call-up by England for the final Test against West Indies at The Oval, the end of another unsuccessful series. The selectors were operating on a whim and a prayer and anyone who had done well in the championship had a chance of playing, regardless of whether those in charge believed they had the ability and temperament to succeed. It was trial and error, the triumph of hope over expectation, and if you did not shape up immediately, you were shipped out.

The fact I was not chosen for the tour of India that winter – Rob Bailey getting the nod over me for a trip which ended up being called off – was proof that I was either called up as a pointer for the future, or to appease commentators in the media who had been pushing my name forward. I only made 13 runs in that match at The Oval. No one spoke to me afterwards. I came, failed to conquer and went. I had not made the immediate impact that was required in those days, but neither did I enjoy much luck.

I was dismissed for three in my first innings, caught behind by Jeffrey Dujon at the third attempt trying to cut Curtly Ambrose. In the second, I had made 10, passing 1,000 runs for the season with a four off Winston Benjamin, when I was dismissed in bizarre fashion. A delivery from Benjamin hit my pad and rebounded onto my bat, offering Benjamin a return catch which he held on to after a juggling act. Ian Botham said he had never seen anything like it. I was then dropped for the final Test of the season against Sri Lanka at Lord's: good enough to play against the best team in the world, but not against international cricket's newcomers. Kim Barnett was called up for his first cap and Allan Lamb returned. I had been another lamb to the slaughter.

West Indies won the series 4–0 and England had gone a record 18 Test matches without a victory. Four captains were used in the five matches: Mike Gatting, John Emburey, Chris Cowdrey and Graham Gooch. David Gower found himself leading the side the following summer against Australia as more heads rolled. Players didn't turn up for England matches then in cars, so much as tumbrils.

Not surprisingly, there was little spirit or camaraderie in the England dressing-room. With 28 players used in the six Tests that summer, it was more like a halfway house than a point of arrival, and there was little in the way of self-belief. To survive, players had to play for themselves because the team was not going anywhere. It encouraged individuality and selfishness to the point where the team ethic disappeared over the boundary and ensured that England's failure was self-perpetuating. The surprise was that it continued for so long with the blame for the decline attributed to the county system. All I can say is that Australia would have made far better use of it because they looked for reasons while we came up with excuses.

I started the 1989 season not having a clue where I stood with England. By chance in April, I bumped into the England manager, Micky Stewart, at a hotel in Leicester where he was having breakfast. He told me that if I started well for Glamorgan I would have an excellent chance of being involved in the Ashes series against Australia that summer. He told me to keep going and he watched me at Leicester, where I was over-shadowed by David Gower who scored a career-best 228.

Two weeks later, I made the highest score of my career, an unbeaten 191 against Gloucestershire in Cardiff. I had been 45 not out at the close of play on the second day and that night I went to a barbecue with the Glamorgan spinner Phil North. We ended up drinking more than we had intended on what was a balmy summer evening and the following day we found ourselves batting together, just as we had done on my championship début. Phil hung around long enough then for me to get my century, but he couldn't quite manage it for my double-ton.

We put on 54 for the eighth wicket and I was 12 short of 200 when Phil had a heave and was dismissed. He apologised afterwards, saying he was so drained that he barely had the strength to pick up his bat and he wanted to get into the pavilion for a lie down. David Lawrence mopped up the tail to leave me high and dry, but I was more than happy because, taking Micky Stewart at his word, I felt I had a chance for the Ashes. It was not to be, however, and Derbyshire's Kim Barnett was preferred to me in what was to prove another humiliating series for England.

That June I got a telephone call from David Graveney, the Gloucestershire spinner who had been part of the attack I had taken apart in Cardiff. Would I be interested in touring South Africa that winter with an unofficial England team? My instinct was to say yes immediately, despite the five-year ban from international cricket that would have followed, because the money which was being offered – £83,000 over two years after tax – was too good to turn down. I had negotiated an improved contract with Glamorgan after winning my England cap, pleased to get a five-year deal which offered me security even if I lost out financially (because it meant my pay was fixed for a long period).

Gravs brought Ali Bacher, the head of South African cricket, round to see me; my wife, Sue, cooked him a meal at our house. The negotiations were being conducted secretly, but I know my county colleague Greg Thomas had been approached too. Mike Gatting was to be the captain and I spoke to cricketers I respected like Rodney Ontong and Geoff Holmes. They told me to go for it. If I'd thought that I had a chance of getting back into the England squad, I would have deliberated long and hard about the offer, but Stewart had not spoken to me since Leicester and I followed the England example by looking after myself.

Bacher and Graveney told me to keep scoring runs to raise my profile, but my season fell apart as the news started to leak out about the tour and who was going. It created a pressure I could not cope with and, after a run of low scores, Alan Butcher picked me for the reserves. I got my 1,000 runs for the season, but my score against Gloucestershire inflated my average which anyway was less than 28 and I only scored three half-centuries.

On the day that the squad – which included Tim Robinson, Neil Foster, Bill Athey, Paul Jarvis, Graham Dilley and John Emburey – was announced, I was playing for Glamorgan in a Sunday League match against Surrey at The Oval and I was booed onto the pitch. I had just returned from a charity match in Jesmond where a number of the 'rebels' were taking on a West Indies XI. It was virtually known then who would be going to South Africa and Michael Holding showed what he thought of my decision by bowling distinctly quicker against me than he had done when I'd faced him against Derbyshire a couple of weeks earlier.

When Glamorgan played Sussex in Swansea that August, Peter Hain organised a demonstration outside the ground. It started at 10.30 a.m. but I had arrived long before that. I received abuse at a few grounds, but I did not receive the hate mail that I thought my decision would generate. The Glamorgan secretary, Phil Carling, looked for a sponsor who would pay me not to go, but one never materialised. I told him anyway that I wanted to take my place, partly because England had treated me badly with the long-awaited qualification of the Zimbabwean Graeme Hick looming, and also because the money would make me financially secure.

That winter Glamorgan signed Viv Richards, who had turned down several tempting offers to tour South Africa because of his hatred for the apartheid system there. Before our opening championship match of the season against Leicestershire, I sat down and had a chat with Viv because I did not want the fact that I had gone on the tour to be a problem between us – especially as we were likely to be batting together several times over the course of the summer. He told me not to worry and reminded me that at my age he had done something similar when he had signed up for Kerry Packer's World Series, principally for the money. He, too, had been banned by his country. We put on 186 together in the second innings against Leicestershire, the start of a successful partnership.

The money was certainly important: Paul Jarvis worked out that to earn the amount we were receiving from the South Africans, we would have to play every match for England for six years. But, if looking back now I'm not convinced that I made the *wrong* decision, I probably didn't make it for the *right* reasons. I did not think about the political situation in South Africa, naïvely thinking that part of our role was to help raise the profile of the game in the townships, whereas we turned out to be pawns in a political game. South Africa were desperate to end their isolation from Test cricket and they ended up cancelling the second leg of our tour, having shown the International Cricket Council the disruption they could cause. Their readmission quickly followed.

We left in January 1990 with a documentary film crew in tow. There was a certain amount of tension and when we were asked what we would do if Nelson Mandela – who had been a political prisoner for 27 years – was released, Bill Athey tried to lighten the mood by saying, 'It doesn't matter: he can't bat or bowl.' Our flight was delayed for three hours because of a bomb scare and Mike Gatting, who grew in stature over the coming months, took the microphone to apologise to the other passengers.

There were reports of wild scenes at the airport in Johannesburg with an army of protesters waiting to greet us, but because our flight was delayed we did not see any of it and got to our hotel in Sandton without any disruption. I wandered down to the bar after unpacking and a big Afrikaans guy, some 6ft 4in. tall and almost as broad, came up to me and asked who I was. I was on my guard and merely replied, 'Matthew.'

'It's Maynard, isn't it?' he said in reply. 'I'm Gerhardus and I am here to look after you.' The South Africans had provided a special police force to protect us. Gerhardus had a gun tucked down behind his back and he had the most incredible knife I had ever seen, designed to stick out from a clenched fist. Quick for slitting throats, he told me. He said he had used it a couple of times – not a guy to get on the wrong side of. Gerhardus and his mates were all keep-fit fanatics and Bill Athey and I used to play touch rugby with them most days, machine guns marking out the try-lines and M-16s acting as touchlines. Not surprisingly, the parks where we played were deserted.

We were meant to play two Test and seven one-day internationals, but the itinerary was cut back because of the protests we attracted. At one, in Pietermaritzburg, there was a crowd of some 4,000 and a real danger of violence breaking out. Gatt was determined to say why we were out there, but our protection crew advised him against saying a word. Gatt was not put off and he pushed through the crowd to get to the microphone. He said we were there to play cricket, not make a political statement, and that our presence in South Africa in no way meant that we condoned apartheid. He calmed the mood, but a bomb in a Cape Town club owned by the former England player Bob Woolmer meant the tour was cut short and we only played one Test.

I ended up playing in only four matches, a two-day game against South African Universities and three one-day internationals. I failed to reach double figures in all of my five innings and I ended up being paid more than £5,000 a run. I was the youngest player in the squad and I suppose the one with the most to lose in terms of a prospective international career, but I hardly justified my place on the tour and my last innings summed it up: bowled (Allan) Donald, duck.

Nelson Mandela was released when we were in South Africa and the scenes were incredible, with impromptu street parties called everywhere. The white management team at our hotel had to do all the cooking and cleaning and it was all an eye-opener to me. At 23, I had had little experience of the wide world and my life tended to revolve around cricket. It gave me a wider perspective and I became more questioning. I was out there for ten weeks and it was a valuable part of my growing up process, far more worthwhile than looking for a job in Wales during the winter to supplement my cricket income.

I never once feared for my life, though we were not the most popular of visitors to the country. One night when we were in Johannesburg, we went to a Greek restaurant after persistent pleading from the owner. Gatt took a few of us along and we quickly got into a relaxed mood, giving our orders and sampling the local wine. The place was packed, which was why, we thought, the food was taking so long to arrive. But the owner seemed to be knocking back too much ouzo and was growing redder and redder in the face. Eventually he came to our table and said, 'I am very sorry, Mr Gatting. You will not be getting any food because all my staff have walked out in protest at your presence here.' The man was in a right state because half his other customers had not had their food either and he did not know if his staff would ever return. 'This could finish me,' he said, pouring himself another restorative.

Gatt, typically, took charge – aware, I think, that he was the player whom the staff had recognised. He told the owner to pull himself together and asked how much steak he had. He ordered Paul Jarvis and me to act as waiters and go round the tables asking the other diners whether they minded having steak for their supper and how they wanted it cooked. Gatt went into the kitchens and started grilling every piece of steak he could find in the fridge. The vegetables had already been prepared and as Gatt slapped the meat onto plates, Paul and I piled on the veg and took the food outside to the tables.

Gatt emerged to a standing ovation and the owner, in typical Greek fashion, celebrated by smashing all the plates (well, there was no way we were going to do the washing up as well). He was barely able to stand by the end, but he still had enough about him to realise that he might not be opening on the following day. We rang him that lunchtime: all his staff had returned and boom was not going to turn to bust.

The cricket was far tougher than Gatt's steaks. South Africa, on their own for so long, had a point to prove and they won the Test, with Allan Donald showing signs of things to come. We needed Neil Foster to bowl at his best, but he was all over the place. At the end of the third day, he asked someone to bat against him in the nets but failed to find any takers. Unimpressed, he said he would bowl at a can. 'Better take a skip full, then,' said Jarvis. Everyone creased up and Foster stormed out. He didn't bowl well that match, but of all the bowlers I have faced in my career, he is without any doubt in the top ten.

I had hoped to make an impact on the harder wickets in South Africa, but my technique had gone to pot after the shocking way I ended the 1989 season. I changed my guard, but it only put doubts in my mind about where my stumps were and I did not know where my next run was coming from. With so much experience in the squad, I found myself on the margins and it was clear before we went home that the tour the following year was not going to take place.

The tour meant I would not be qualified to play for England again until 1995, though the five-year ban turned into one of 18 months after South Africa regained their place on the ICC. Rob Bailey had been asked to go to South Africa, but he turned down the chance so as not to wreck his international prospects. He went on the 1991 tour to West Indies, where he was given out caught down the leg-side after a typically menacing appeal from Viv Richards. The ball had hit Rob on the thigh pad, but Viv panicked the umpire and Rob never played for England again. So much for loyalty: had England had a more coherent selection policy, I am not sure that the South Africa tour would have happened and there would certainly have been far fewer capped players to tempt away.

The tour did not have an adverse effect on my career. I enjoyed a successful summer in 1990 as Glamorgan, under the leadership of Alan Butcher, at last showed signs of competing consistently. Sue and I bought a house in Pentyrch, a village on the outskirts of Cardiff, with the money I had earned – a big step up from the property we'd had on a large estate near Llandaff – without having to increase our mortgage. Bacher and his South African cricket board had paid a seven-figure sum to get the 'rebel' squad over, paying us for a tour we were not to make, but he ended up getting what he wanted and in the end we proved to be a relatively cheap investment.

7. OVER HERE

One of the reasons given for the decline of the England team from the 1980s has been the presence of overseas players in the county game. In the early 1970s, counties could sign as many stars from abroad as they could afford, but that quickly changed as things were seen to get out of hand. When I started to play for Glamorgan, counties were allowed to register two overseas players, but only one could play in a first-class match. Today, sides are allowed to have only one non-European Union player under contract.

I believe that number should be restored to two. We have had some unsuccessful signings from abroad at Glamorgan, but equally we have had our successes. The recruitment of Viv Richards in 1990 boosted our membership considerably, as did the Pakistan fast bowler Waqar Younis in 1997. Players of that quality lift a dressing-room and help stimulate interest in a county. I do not see how it can be argued at the same time that there are too many mediocre players in county cricket and that overseas recruits are holding back British youngsters. You cannot have it both ways.

I only played with Javed Miandad a couple of times, but he played a major role in my development as a batsman. Viv lifted the level of our performance through his professionalism. Waqar played a major part in our 1997 championship success. The Australian Test opener Matthew Elliott played crucial innings to help us win promotion to the first division of the championship in 2000. And the Indian all-rounder Ravi Shastri, who had two spells with us between 1987 and 1991, was an important signing as we looked to turn ourselves into a more hard-nosed side.

Ravi was a genuine all-rounder who would have got into the side on the strength of his batting or bowling alone, though by the end of his stint with us his bowling action had gone completely. He never recovered after being persistently reverse-swept by Dermot Reeve at Warwickshire, and when we subsequently played Leicestershire, he was sending down double bouncers. He had bowled for years in Test cricket, but he suddenly developed an attack of the yips which no amount of bowling in the nets could cure. However his batting more than justified his place in the side, as befitted a player who had equalled Sir Gary Sobers's record of six sixes in one over – though not for us.

Ravi was single in those days and a real ladies' man. He would carry a little black book with him and when we played away, he would stroll into the commentary box of the BBC Radio Wales cricket reporter Edward Bevan and beg to use his telephone (this was the pre-mobile-phone era). One time, a few of us were sitting in Edward's box at Edgbaston when Ravi breezed in and asked if he could make a call and, no, he was not ringing his family back in India. We were going on to Leeds from Birmingham and Ravi had arrangements to make. He pulled out his little book and dialled a number, which was clearly a work one. Whoever answered the telephone told Ravi that the woman he had asked for was not there. Ravi then asked for a home number. When he was told that was against company policy, he asked if a message could be relayed telling her that Ravi Shastri of Glamorgan and India would be at a certain hotel in Leeds on Saturday night. Suddenly, a confused look came over his face and he put the phone down quietly.

He sat silent for a few moments and then asked: 'What is maternity leave?' After we had explained and then recovered from laughing, he shook his head, muttered 'Oh dear', took out his pen and crossed out the number. On the Saturday night, he pitched up with a striking woman on his arm. One of the players recognised her, claiming to have seen Ravi's companion on page three of a red-top tabloid that week.

In 1988, Ravi helped us enjoy our best one-day season for several years with his ability to accelerate quickly at the end of an innings. He was a tall, lean man who had a cultured technique, but when the occasion demanded he batted with an astonishing ferocity. We played one match at a new outground in 1989, taking Middlesex to the charms of the Hoover Sports Ground in Merthyr Tydfil. Hugh Morris was the captain and when he went out to inspect the pitch his thumb disappeared as he dug it into the turf.

All of a sudden there was a loud voice: 'Hey, Morris, what do you think? This is the hardest wicket we have had here for 20 years.' It was the groundsman, clearly proud of his work, while the batsmen were looking for excuses to drop down the order, knowing that the soft surface would favour the bowlers. Middlesex not surprisingly put us into bat after winning the toss and we struggled. Enter Ravi: he put on 73 for the fourth wicket with Geoff Holmes, whose contribution was nine, and he hit six sixes and six fours in his 92 – a record for Glamorgan against Middlesex in the Sunday League. We won the match comfortably.

In 1990, we registered the young West Indies fast bowler Hamesh Anthony along with Viv. He had been recommended to us as a player to watch and, after turning down the chance to sign Michael Holding in the 1970s when he was an unknown in favour of Gregory Armstrong, Glamorgan did not want to miss out again. Hamesh had a second stint with us in 1995 when our then overseas player, Ottis Gibson, was touring Britain with West Indies, but by then his promise had not materialised. Hamesh never appeared too keen on the Welsh weather and it is not unfair to say that he was not the sharpest tool in the box. In 1995 we had put him in a plush flat full of all the mod cons not far from the ground at Sophia Gardens. Hamesh came to training one morning shaking his head and complaining that he was hungry. He had bought a pizza the previous night and had stuck it in what he thought was the microwave. It turned out to be the washing machine.

Ottis was relatively unknown when he joined us in 1994 but went on to be capped by West Indies. When the mood took him he was a quick and hostile bowler; but he soon wearied of the slow wickets at Cardiff and in his final year with us in 1996 only took one wicket in Wales, for 350 runs. He did more for us with the bat, a hard hitter lurking in the lower middle order who showed the virtue of playing straight. He could have developed into a genuine all-rounder, but I am not sure how hungry he was for success. There were times when he had batsmen hopping around, but unless there was something in the wicket, he quickly lost interest.

My first full season as Glamorgan captain was in 1996. I felt we were almost good enough to challenge for the championship, but we needed a signing like Viv, a leading name to show to supporters and the rest of the country how ambitious we were. Jonathan Barnett, an agent, that summer submitted a list of overseas players he had on his books: would we be interested in signing any of them? The name which leaped out was that of Waqar Younis who, with his fellow Pakistani fast bowler Wasim Akram, had pioneered the art of reverse swing. Waqar was one of the leading bowlers in the world and he had had a successful career with Surrey. Interested? Barnett did not know the half of it. Mike Fatkin, the Glamorgan secretary, and I took the train to London to meet Waqar and Barnett and a deal was reached quickly.

Surrey were keen to re-sign Waqar, but he was still upset about the way he had been treated by them previously. Like Viv, he liked the idea of living and playing a long way from London and enjoying some privacy. Mike and Barnett didn't take long to agree the financial side of the contract, which included a significant bonus element. I felt that Waqar was the one piece in the jigsaw we were missing, a genuine pace bowler who could run through sides, and Mike and I had a few beers on the train coming back. He pulled rank and delegated me to do the television interviews when we got back to Cardiff, volunteering himself to go on radio.

There was an unhappy sequel. Ottis was clearly not going to be retained and Glamorgan also decided to release some other players at the end of the summer, including Steve Barwick, a wily bowler who had been with the club for 15 years. Unfortunately, the club told the players before the end of the season that their contracts would not be renewed; during the final Second XI match against Worcester at Barnt Green, Baz and Andrew Dalton refused to take any further part in the match, while Neil Kendrick expressed his disgust to the club in forthright terms.

Kendrick was a slow left-arm bowler whom we had signed from Surrey in 1995, but his chances were going to be limited because of the emergence of Dean Cosker. I was sorry to see Neil go, because he had fitted in well into the dressing-room. Before one match against his old county, he asked us to give him a few Welsh words he could hurl at the Surrey players who would know they were being insulted but would not know how to respond. Neil spent a few sessions yelling *'hufen ia'* at the batsmen. We'd not told him what it meant, only that it was language not to be used in public. It was only later that we explained to him he had been shouting at his former team-mates, 'Ice-cream'. And it was a scream.

The players whose contracts were not being renewed had every right to feel aggrieved because the timing was poor, but they mimicked the club by behaving unprofessionally. Baz had been a close friend of mine, but I have not spoken to him since then. He has turned down invitations to attend the weddings of players and, to my knowledge, he has only been to Glamorgan once – at Swansea, in 2000, when he stayed away from the dressing-room area.

Everyone blames someone, but I felt the time had come to let Baz go. He had been a top bowler for Glamorgan, opening the bowling in his early years before refining his action and sending down wily off-cutters which constricted batsmen and made him particularly effective in one-day cricket. But in his latter years with us, the opposition had started to work him out. As he used his bat to lean on and was not the best of fielders, it became harder to justify his place in the first-team squad, but there was actually a greater concern to me.

Baz was a throwback, in that he had little time for modern fitness methods. On one pre-season tour, we were having a net and up he sauntered, in a tracksuit, with a fag in his mouth. He sent down three deliveries, all on the spot, pulled a hamstring and retired, his pre-season over. He liked a drink after a day's play and was often the last to bed, but he knew his capacity and was invariably first up for breakfast. While he could look after himself, I was worried about the influence he was having on Darren Thomas, a promising fast bowler who had taken five wickets on his championship début against Derbyshire as a 17-year-old, but who was losing his way and was in danger of being shown the door.

Hugh Morris's response when he was captain in 1995 had been to impose a 10 p.m. curfew on Darren, a sanction I did not support. It was too authoritarian and rigid. My approach to captaincy was more consensual and I would have thought that Hugh would have learnt his lesson after an incident in 1987. We had lost to Yorkshire heavily in a NatWest Trophy match at Headingley, shot out for 84 after being put in. Hugh carried his bat for 16 with only Greg Thomas keeping him company for more than a few minutes and the game was nearly over before lunch.

Hugh was not amused and when we returned to Yorkshire later in the season to play in the championship, he imposed a 9.30 p.m. curfew on the players. Everyone had to be back in the hotel by that time each night. It did not go down well with the players and, after a couple of early nights, there was a rebellion. Hugh was chatting in the corner of the hotel bar with his fellow opener John 'Ponty' Hopkins at 10 p.m. one night. The rest of us indulged in some exaggerated yawning and left as if to go to our rooms.

We bolted to a club and were getting the frustration out of our system and enjoying a beer when who should walk in but Hugh and John Hopkins. There was nothing Hugh could say because he and Ponty had decided to take advantage of our early night by sneaking out of the hotel. Hugh lost a lot of respect in the eyes of the players after that and I learned from that experience when I took over as captain. You have to trust players to look after themselves because they know their own limits: everyone is different.

The problem with Darren Thomas was that Baz had taken him under his wing. When I started with Glamorgan, Ian Smith was a promising young all-rounder but he fell in with the wrong crowd and ended up socialising to excess. He eventually moved to Durham, but never really made it and I didn't want the same thing happening to Darren. The solution, to me, lay not in telling Darren when he had to be tucked up in bed: Baz was coming to the end of his career at the age of 36 and in a way he was holding Darren back, both by taking up a place in the team and by socialising. The club decided not to renew Baz's contract.

I should have been the one to tell him why, but after the Glamorgan committee had made the decision, Alan Jones was sent up to Barnt Green to tell him and the others the bad news. It was something I found painful because Baz had been part of the fixtures and fittings in our dressing-room for so long. He had provided a shoulder for me to cry on in 1994 after my experiences with England in the Caribbean and he had a lot to offer young players. His knowledge of cricket was limitless, he was acute at working out the strengths and weaknesses of batsmen and he could have helped Darren in that sense. The problem was that he kept Darren up too late and it showed the following day. Darren was in danger of drinking his career away. Something had to be done.

Darren has not looked back since. From a player in danger of being made redundant, he played a major role in our 1997 championship success, won his county cap and went on two England A tours. He was a captain's dream, always ready and willing when called on. In our final championship of the 2000 season against Middlesex in Cardiff, when we needed a draw to win promotion to the first division, Darren insisted on playing despite a groin injury which made him walk with a limp. He gave it everything on the final day and was rewarded with the wicket which took us up.

As the 1997 campaign neared its end, I had a quiet chat with Waqar Younis. We had two matches to go: two victories would guarantee us the championship. Waqar enjoyed the nightlife in Cardiff and would often club it into the small hours. I asked him, for the good of the team, to calm down a bit until we had the title in the bag. I did not order him to, just quietly made my point, and he took the message on board.

Waqar was a great signing for us. Injury meant he had to return home early in 1998, but he had delivered the previous year, winning two consecutive matches for us after we had been bowled out by Middlesex for 31 in Cardiff. Despite his status in the game as one of the world's leading fast bowlers, Waqar was as ambitious for success at Glamorgan as I was and his presence often unnerved the opposition. We were playing at Kent early in the 1997 season and Waqar was giving David Fulton a torrid time and there was a lot of playing and missing.

'You haven't got a clue, have you?' said Waqar to Fulton after coming down the wicket, having seen a ball just miss the off stump. Waqar walked slowly back to his mark, a fair distance, leaving Fulton to sweat. The next ball was his trademark yorker and the middle stump went flying out of the ground. Exit Fulton and how much better it made us feel to have a bowler of Waqar's quality in the side.

The South African all-rounder Jacques Kallis took over from Waqar as our overseas player in 1999. He only played the final third of the season, because of the World Cup and injury, but he quickly made an impact. He hit an unbeaten 155 against Surrey in the Sunday League at Pontypridd, one month after they had skittled us for 44 at The Oval. He fitted quickly into the team, enjoying coming out for a beer after a day's play, and he set an example to the younger players when it came to fitness, introducing a new series of warming-down techniques. He was someone everyone looked up to.

Jacques is probably the leading all-rounder in the world today, a batsman going in at number three and a fast bowler who sends the ball down at around 90 mph. He was contracted to return to Glamorgan for the 2001 season – however, a problem with recruiting overseas players has cropped up recently, for whereas only England used to play home Test matches during the British summer, more and more international fixtures are now being arranged in May, August and September and this makes signing big names more hazardous.

When we signed Matthew Elliott for the 2000 campaign, he was on the fringe of the Australian squad, having played 20 Tests. Before the end of the season he had been offered a national contract after proving himself a match-winner for us. He was different to Jacques, not so keen on fitness sessions because of a knee injury, but he was a big believer in nets and he brought the Australian mentality of winning to the dressing-room. He'd played a couple of games for us when he asked, 'How do you guys celebrate a win?' Having a few beers and more was not always an option because of the travelling and Matt asked whether we had a team song. We didn't, but it gave our opening bowler Owen Parkin (who fancied himself as a lyricist with lines like 'Steve James Superstar; scores more runs than Mark Butcher', with 'Butcher' made to rhyme with 'superstar') an idea and within a day he had come up with the 12-line chant which we now ritually sing after every victory.

The first time we sang it was after we had beaten Hampshire in the quarter-final of the Benson & Hedges Cup in Cardiff. We were warbling away as Robin Smith, the Hampshire captain and a good mate of mine, came to our dressing-room for the presentation ceremony only to hear us chanting 'Over the Severn and down to the Taff'. I apologised to him because we had not wanted to cause offence to his side. Hampshire are a good bunch of guys, but when we beat Surrey in the semi-final, we were only too keen for them to hear every word.

Robin's reaction was typical of the man: he liked the idea and I would not be surprised if more and more counties do not adopt their own song in the coming years. We have been trend-setters before: we were the first side to adopt a defined dress code for all match days from 1997 and a lot of teams copied that. Matt Elliott's legacy to Glamorgan will be lasting, never mind that he once cried over spilt orange juice.

Matt recognised that a team gets strength from the dressing-room and there were times that season when, if we were struggling in the field, someone would start singing our song and immediately there was an edge again. When I look back at the overseas players Glamorgan have had in my time, I would definitely raise the permitted number to two if I had the power. It would require the ICC to limit the amount of international cricket being played in a calendar year and there are far too many meaningless one-day tournaments being arranged.

As I have argued before, Glamorgan would not have enjoyed success in the 1990s had it not been for the example set by Viv Richards. With cricket not played at any decent level in the rest of Europe, there would be no danger of the counties being swamped by players unqualified to play for England, as is the case with soccer, and there would be at least nine places for British players in each side put out by the 18 first-class counties. That makes 162 players – more than enough.

8. PICKING UP THE PIECES

After returning home from South Africa before the start of the 1990 season, I did not need to worry about impressing the England selectors, for I had put myself in international isolation. Perhaps it was just coincidence, but I then enjoyed my best two seasons for Glamorgan. I passed 1,500 runs in each of them and in 1991 I at last converted half-centuries into three-figure scores: seven centuries against five fifties in an aggregate of 1,803 runs.

The arrival of Viv Richards had helped, but the summer of 1990 was a vintage one for batting all round the country. Six Glamorgan batsmen passed 1,000 runs, the second-highest total in the club's history, and we compiled 30 centuries, compared to the previous best of 17 in 1981 and 1985. Alan Butcher became the first England-qualified batsman to reach 1,000 runs for the second successive year, but we were also on the receiving end: Jimmy Cook's unbeaten 313 for Somerset in Cardiff was the highest individual score ever made against Glamorgan.

The previous summer had been one for the bowlers when there had been an experiment with a ball which had a pronounced seam. A crop of low-scoring matches led to that ball being ditched and this, together with 25-point penalties handed out to Essex and Nottinghamshire for preparing substandard pitches (a sanction which cost Essex the championship title) ensured that 1990 was a year for batsmen. Only Sussex reached 60 batting points in 1989 and no county secured more batting than bowling bonus points: ten sides passed that total a year later and only five teams secured more bowling than batting points.

Viv Richards topped our averages with 61.95. It would have been good enough to top the list in 1989, but in 1990 it did not merit a place in the top 20. Tom Moody hit the fastest century of the season against us at St Helen's. It took him just 26 minutes, though it was less the pitch that made it easy for him and more six overs from yours truly which went for 89 runs as Butch indulged in some declaration bowling – or flighted filth, as someone called it. It worked because we won, but there was an endemic problem of wickets which too often held little to interest the bowlers, meaning that contrived finishes abounded. The eventual upshot was the introduction of four-day cricket, a move which quickly led to result wickets being prepared so that a number of matches finished long before the start of the fourth day.

In my 16 years as a county cricketer there has been constant chopping and changing. The championship was increased to 18 counties with the introduction of Durham in 1992; the number of fixtures for each side was reduced from 24 to 22 and then 17; the bonus points system has been overhauled several times; points for a draw were introduced to discourage losing sides from folding with little resistance so they could get on the road early; and then came the split into two divisions. This last move I opposed because I couldn't see how a competition might logically become more competitive if only nine sides, rather than eighteen, could win the championship title.

These changes sum up the muddled thinking of the Test and County Cricket Board which mutated in the late 1990s into the England and Wales Cricket Board. Glamorgan were the only county to vote against the move to two divisions in the County Championship. I was told by one member of our committee – who should have known better – not to worry, because if the reform did not work out, the board would go back to the old system. I scoffed in disbelief: it was a change which was going to alter the face of the county game permanently, but the 'blazers' could not see it. I suppose they were used to sticking their fingers in the dyke, but they did not have a vision for the future and could not appreciate that sacred cows such as an equal share-out of Test match receipts between the counties, and prohibition of transfers of players who were under contract, were going to come under severe pressure as success became more and more important.

My fear is that within five or ten years the second division will be seen as second class, with counties in it forced to go part-time. I cannot see the system of three up and three down at the end of each season surviving. There were murmurings after the end of the first year about how you could justify the demotion of a third of the sides in the first division. It isn't difficult to predict what will happen: there will be moves to reduce the number of relegated to two clubs, then perhaps one, and there will end up being such a difference between the two divisions that calls will be made for ring-fencing.

There were two conflicting arguments for two divisions. The first was that it would benefit the England side; the second was that it would make county cricket more commercial by raising competitiveness and stimulating interest. So what did the England and Wales Cricket Board do? Introduce the two-division system at the same time as it put leading England players under central contracts, leaving the national coach with the power to pull them out of county matches as he sees fit.

I believe that central contracts are long overdue and the system should be extended to include more players. But a county which is in danger of being relegated is not going to welcome its leading player or players being told to stand down for a crucial match. Sides will build up their squads to ensure they have strength in depth and that will put pressure on the game's registration system. The first transfer fee for a cricketer is not that far away.

The first-class game is in a mess because it is largely controlled by amateurs – with Glamorgan a prime example. The main reason I gave up the captaincy after five years is that I became so frustrated with having to deal with the Glamorgan committee. Seeing trivial matters inflated to something as serious as life and death started killing my enjoyment of the game. Even Hugh Morris, far more of an establishment figure than me, used to come out of committee meetings with a fierce look in his eyes.

The committee is more numerous than our first-team squad, far more so, and a number of them have no experience of running a first-class side. When Glamorgan played Zimbabwe at St Helen's in 1985 Graeme Hick was, in a sign of things to come, taking our attack apart. I was not playing in the match, but a senior figure on the committee came into the dressing-room at the lunch interval to give the players the benefit of his advice.

'If I were you ,' he said, 'I would bowl at Hick for run-outs. Put your mid-on back ten yards.' Thank you very much Albert Einstein. There are ways of dealing with committees: Duncan Fletcher was superb when he was at Glamorgan, showing little emotion as he seethed inside, and the committee loved him. I was neither as patient nor as tolerant and by the end it became too much of a battle. I wanted to give the captaincy up after the 1999 season and concentrate on my batting after an average season, but the club had appointed the Australian Jeff Hammond to succeed Fletch as coach and it would not have been ideal to have had a new captain as well.

At the start of the 1999 season, I had chosen David Harrison, an 18-year old all-rounder, to make his début in our first championship match against Derbyshire. The selection was a hunch after I had seen David bowl in the nets: he was tall, he bowled at a useful pace, generating movement and bounce, and he was a useful batsman. It meant leaving out the more experienced Owen Parkin, but I was always one to back my judgement rather than stick to a plan. Fletch backed me and I told Parky that he had been left out, and why.

Parky approached Hugh Davies, then the chairman of Glamorgan's cricket committee and someone I didn't have the best of relationships with. Hugh told Parky that he would have a word with me. He should have told Owen that selection had nothing to do with the cricket committee and that if he had a problem he should see me: that was my response to the player when I found out what he had done. Instead, Hugh came up to me and said that the committee would like to be forewarned in future about any surprise selections I might be inclined to make.

Hugh had stuck his oar in before. His son, Adam, was a promising young fast bowler who was quite close to getting a full contract and his family interest made things awkward. I told Hugh that if the committee wanted to know about selections in advance, they should come down to the nets and watch the reserves in action – then they would not be bothered by the element of surprise, because they would know who was in form and who was not. After a subsequent disagreement, I volunteered to hand over the selecting of the side to the cricket committee: they felt that they knew the best team, so let them pick it. The bluff worked and they generally kept their opinions to themselves after that.

Victories over the committee were rarer than defeats. The loss which most upset me was when Tony Cottey joined Sussex at the end of the 1998 season. Cotts had been my vice-captain for two years and he was three years away from being entitled to his Benefit. He wanted a three-year contract to take him through to his Benefit year. The committee offered him two and Hugh Davies refused to budge. That made Cotts, not the tallest of men, feel very small: he was then 32 and, a former professional soccer player with Swansea City, he was one of the fittest players in the squad. It was typical of the way an amateur deals with a professional. It's absurd that while the game has become more and more professional on the field to the point where the new generation of players have little in common with their predecessors, it is still run by blazers who are only too prominent when things are going well but cannot be sighted when the going gets rough. The concession of the Glamorgan committee to the modern era was to decrease its size from 28 members to 24. Half of them, at least, have no contribution to make; but the likelihood of getting a board of directors to run the club is remote because the committee would have to self-destruct. No chance of that happening.

Cotts never got his three-year deal, despite Fletch pleading his case as well as me. He joined Sussex on a five-year contract, earning a lot more annually than he had done at Glamorgan, but he will end up losing overall because he will not get a Benefit. He would not have gone had he felt wanted. Gerard Elias, a QC, took over as chairman and tried to get to know the players by speaking to them individually. He asked Cotts why he was inconsistent: 'If I knew that,' came the reply, 'I wouldn't be.' And I thought that barristers were not meant to ask questions unless they had a very good idea what the answer would be.

Elias did his best to keep Cotts. He faced an almost impossible task, because neither Hugh Davies nor Cottey would want to be seen to be losing face having dug their heels in for so long. Elias offered to guarantee Cotts a third year, promising that even if he were not a first-team regular (he had been left out in 1997 and 1998 occasionally for the promising Mike Powell), he would be the Second XI captain. It was a clever compromise, but Cotts took it the wrong way and was advised to leave by a player who should have known better. He had won his cap in the same year as Robert Croft, Steve James and Adrian Dale and felt he would definitely lose out on his Benefit.

So we ended up losing another experienced player from our championship-winning side, with Hugh Morris retired and Waqar Younis out of contract. I was angry that he had been allowed to go, because he had been the perfect foil to me as vice-captain: he had a deep knowledge of the game and saw things from a different perspective to me. He has never scored any runs against us for Sussex. He's left us in body, but not in spirit!

The incident made me determined that 1999 would be my last season as captain. I enjoyed leading the side, but battling with the committee wearied me mentally and my form started to suffer. I know that the committee were wary of appointing me as captain in 1996. I should have had the job three years before that, after leading the side for virtually the whole of the 1992 season. I was Alan Butcher's vice-captain then and he only played three matches that year because of a knee injury which finished his career. I know that he recommended that I take over from him as skipper, but the appointment was in the gift of the committee. No one applied: it was merely offered.

When I joined the club, I had no real ambition to be captain one day. But my eyes were opened by the way Butch led the side. He was shrewd and competitive, not afraid to make tough decisions. Success was his motivation and he dropped me to the reserves after a bad run. In the three seasons from 1990, I had established myself as one of the senior players in the side and my experience in South Africa had matured me considerably. I still went for my shots as a batsman, but I saw things from a wider perspective and the captaincy started to appeal to me.

I scored my first double-hundred in 1991 – 204 against Nottinghamshire at Sophia Gardens – and quickly followed it up with 243 against Hampshire at Southampton, which was then the third-highest-ever innings for Glamorgan. We finished 12th in the championship, but we were only 22 points adrift of Kent in sixth place and we were changing as a side, whipping-boys no longer.

We dropped to 14th in 1992 but only lost four matches. One more victory would have taken us into the top half of the table. Considering that Butch only played in two championship matches and that Viv missed nine games because of injury and personal problems, it was a respectable effort. We had won the Tilcon Trophy, a triangular tournament involving Yorkshire and Sussex, and we were building for a brighter future.

The committee met at the end of the season to decide the captaincy. We had won our final championship match of the season, against Derbyshire at Cardiff in a declaration match which had seen both sides forfeit an innings. We set them 308 and, as they fell behind the rate, I bowled a few overs to keep them interested. Robert Croft took 6 for 49 and we won by 63 runs. After the game, their captain Kim Barnett came up to me and congratulated me on my captaincy. If only he had been on the Glamorgan committee.

As the players celebrated the victory that evening, I was at the club waiting to be told who would be the captain for 1993. Hugh Morris got the nod and I think he knew he had it in the bag because at the time the decision was made he was on a train to London. Alan Butcher, Alan Jones, Tony Lewis and Peter Walker, the former Glamorgan and England all-rounder, had all voted for me, but the executive committee went for Hugh. The professionals were on my side, but the amateurs won.

In retrospect, the committee could say they were right because we won the Sunday League under Hugh's captaincy in 1993 – our first trophy for 24 years – and he was far better prepared for the captaincy than he had been in 1986. However the decision still rankles, mainly for the way in which it was done. Peter Walker resigned from the committee in disgust and it meant the end of Butch's time at the club: his playing days were over, but there was no way he was going to remain in a coaching capacity, given his lack of a good relationship with Hugh.

That winter I received a telephone call from Kim: would I be interested in joining Derbyshire? His timing was right because I was still angry at missing out on the captaincy. I had a year to run on my contract with Glamorgan and told Kim that I wouldn't be available until 1994. Derbyshire offered to double my salary and they would pay for my removal fees. I had been tapped up by some other counties before, but on a more informal basis, and I had to think about it.

I had a lot of time for Kim, who is still going strong for

Gloucestershire, and the offer made me take stock. After talking it through with Sue, though, I decided that I would be moving for the wrong reasons. We were settled in Pentyrch and, if the committee were not my natural allies, I felt I had won the respect of the players: there would be another chance to captain the club. The money was tempting and had I not gone to South Africa with the 'rebels' I may well have tilted the other way. It was not until 1999 that my pay packet matched what Derbyshire had offered me.

I told Kim no at the start of the 1993 season, having avoided the temptation to say yes in anger, and it was one of the best decisions I have ever made. I regained my place in the England side that summer and Glamorgan had their best year since 1969. While we were on our way up, Derbyshire were starting a decline; within five years Kim had left them.

9. WINTER SUNSHINE

You do not become a county cricketer for the money. The real rewards in the game only come if you become an established player in an international side, and even then it is small beer compared to what leading soccer players are on – some of whom earn twice as much in a week as some capped cricketers do in a year. When the England rugby squad went on strike in November 2000 in protest at their match fees, it brought home just how far cricket and rugby union are behind soccer, because both sports lack the broad spectator base of football.

Without the international game there would be no full-time professionals in rugby union or cricket. That fact was emphasised at the end of the 2000 season when the England and Wales Cricket Board told counties to expect a £50,000 shortfall each because so many of the Tests between England and West Indies had ended prematurely (in one case, after just two days, though given the batting frailties of both sides, you would have thought that the board would have taken out insurance).

Some of the counties considered cutting back on the number of contracted players on their books and the Professional Cricketers' Association (PCA) became involved. Money is going to become more and more of an issue in the coming years and the PCA needs to be pro-active. The Benefit system for players has been decried, but without it there would be less incentive for a player turning professional, especially if he had a career off the field mapped out, such as law or medicine. There are aspects of a Benefit which can be embarrassing, such as having bucket collections at matches, but there is no way that counties could afford to pay players in lieu of a tax-free Benefit.

In the summer of 1985, the sum of £2,000 seemed a lot of money, especially when Glamorgan provided Ian Smith, Martin Roberts and me accommodation at the National Sports Centre for Wales in Sophia Gardens. It was my first real experience of going away: I knew when I was in Kent for three summers that I would be returning to the Liverpool Arms. If I made it with Glamorgan, Cardiff would become my new home.

We were paid by the club for six months and the cash soon went on socialising. Ian was a social animal and would often come back to our rooms with a smile on his face, armed with a kebab or some other takeaway. He very rarely got through the food and used to throw the leftovers under Martin's bed. Martin was called in to see the Glamorgan secretary Phil Carling one day: the cleaners had made an official complaint about the mess and debris under his bed and he was told to clean up his act or he would be out. Martin apologised to protect Smudger who was banned from bringing any food back. They were happy, carefree months. We were starting out on what we hoped would be a great adventure and often used to play cricket in the corridors. Without family ties, the money was almost incidental to us.

It did mean that winter jobs were essential, though, and I had a variety of these. Despite my lack of culinary skills, I found myself working at a drive-in burger bar in Bangor: I seemed to manage and there were no hamsters around. Then I got a job with Bangor City Football Club whose chairman, John Ross-Jones, was a family friend. I was in the marketing department with the task of persuading pubs to stock our lottery tickets. I used to drive around in a battered Ford Cortina Mk III. It was my pride and joy, but it wouldn't have won any prizes for reliability. I had just stopped off at a pub in Caernarfon one day, only to find that the door lock had jammed when I got back into the car. I had to tie the seat-belt through the door handle and feed it through my arm so that I could steer and change gear without the door flying open.

I got engaged to Sue at the end of 1985 when I was on the dole, having failed to land a job. We had been going out together for more than a year, but I had known her a lot longer than that because she used to work at the Liverpool Arms. We decided to get married at the end of the 1986 season and it turned out that we didn't have to worry about where to go on honeymoon. John Derrick, one of Glamorgan's senior players who went on to become first-team coach, had played in New Zealand for a number of winters and he told me that a club in the area was looking for a professional. Was I interested? Three days after our wedding, and having bought a house in Cardiff, Sue and I flew to Auckland.

I had two thoroughly enjoyable winters with St Joseph's cricket club in Whakatane. We lived near a beach and my job involved spending 20 hours a week coaching in schools. We were met at the airport by the club's chairman, Alan Nielson. He looked like something out of the *Beverly Hillbillies*, with ripped trousers and a moth-ravaged jumper. We feared we would be driving down to the Bay of Plenty on the back of a tractor, as he was an asparagus farmer, but he had a posh car and we looked forward to catching up on some sleep. But Alan was having none of it, pointing out local landmarks before we paid a visit to relatives of Sue's who had emigrated to Auckland. When we eventually got to our house we were told that a party had been laid on in our honour at the club. We were shattered after a journey which had taken some 36 hours door-to-door, but duty called. We slept the whole of the following day.

My last game in the 1986 championship had been at Worcester's New Road, a modern ground, first-class in every respect. My first match in New Zealand was against Opoteki. The club had given me an old Hillman Avenger to drive around in – New Zealand was full of models I thought had gone to the great scrapyard in the sky. It was a brown number with the words 'MATTHEW MAYNARD' printed in bold yellow on the sides, comfortably the worst sponsored car I have ever had, but at the time I was more than grateful for it.

I was driving in it to the first game with Mark Mackinnon, who became a great friend of mine. I asked him where the dressing-rooms were as we got to the ground. 'You're sitting in them,' came the reply. New Road it was not, but a school rugby pitch which had a cricket square cut in its middle. The cricket was not of the highest standard, but it was a good education for me and I found the coaching instructive because it made you search for yourself more.

We had a water bed in the house, which took some getting used to.

It was hard to get the temperature right and it was either too hot or freezing cold. Mind you, Sue and I could have done with it in 1988 when we took off for Australia after I had secured – on Rob Bailey's recommendation – the post of professional with the Gosnells club in Perth. I once played in 44°C heat and our house, which lacked air conditioning, became like a furnace. You would fill a bath with cold water to help you keep cool and within two hours it had turned warm.

There were other British players out in Perth that winter, including Graeme Fowler, Alec Stewart and David Capel, and we used to meet them occasionally. We had an imitation leather sofa, which you slid off when you leaned back. Sue had a nightmare few months there: we had only been in Perth for a couple of weeks when I persuaded her to go to the doctor because she was complaining of headaches and a general feeling of queasiness which I put down to the heat. The doctor said her condition had nothing to do with the weather: Sue was nearly four months pregnant.

We couldn't believe it. Sue had been pregnant earlier in the summer, only to miscarry, and it turned out that she had conceived again almost immediately afterwards. As Sue became advanced, she grew more and more uncomfortable in the heat. The situation meant that I would not be able to stay with Gosnells until the end of March, because the baby was due then. We had flown out on Japan Airlines and they had a limit of eight months for pregnant women on their flights. The club were not happy, but to be fair, we had not gone out there under false pretences. Our son, Tom, duly arrived at the end of March.

The cricket in Perth had been a step up from New Zealand, even though Gosnells did not have any Western Australia players on their books. Matches were played over two days, one week apart. On the first Saturday one side would bat, with the match concluded a week later: 96 overs each and you were allowed, within reason, to change your side for the second day. I had only just arrived when I was asked to help pick the side, having been appointed captain. I replied that there was no point in my having an input because I didn't know anybody. Before our first match, I was berated by a woman who asked me who I thought I was to leave out her son from the side, having only just arrived from Britain. I should be ashamed of myself and I had better not cross her again. When I tried to explain that I had had nothing to do with the selection of the side, it just made her all the more angry and I ended up assuming that I had taken her son's place in the side.

The club had got me a job as a carpenter's assistant. The good news was that the afternoons from 1 p.m. would be my own. The downside was that I had to get up at 5.30 a.m. every morning and, as someone who was like Burlington Bertie (who rose at 10.30), it was hard: hardly the chirpy chappy! The club held nets three nights a week and our house was only 800 metres from the ground. Anyone who failed to turn up, unless they had a genuine reason, was not considered for selection.

Gosnells were a mediocre side – I averaged 40 with the bat and that was comfortably better than anyone else – but the cricket was hard in typically Australian fashion. The wickets were belters and you had to bowl well for your wickets. In one of my early matches our attack was getting flayed and I told the bowlers that they needed to show more aggression. They looked at me uncomprehendingly, so I brought myself on to show them how. Three overs and thirty-three runs later, I retired to the slips and kept my mouth shut.

The following winter, I was in South Africa with the 'rebels'. The year after that I returned to New Zealand to play for Counties, with a view to playing for the Northern Districts. I was with the Papakura club and was selected by the Northern Districts, winning the Shell Trophy with them in my second season. We had an incredible game against Auckland in 1992. Dipak Patel took 12 wickets in the match and scored a double-century, but I received the man-of-the-match award after the game had been drawn. We were 80 for 8 in our first innings and facing the follow-on, when Simon Doull joined me in the middle. We put on more than 200 and I finished with 196. We were set 320 to win, but had to play the game out after I was dismissed for another century. I was determined to hit Patel for six sixes in one over and had managed three before Trevor Franklin, probably the tallest cricketer in New Zealand at the time, caught me on the boundary with his arms outstretched.

I spent the winter of 1992–93 helping Glamorgan with their new membership drive with prices slashed to £15 under the slogan, 'AFFORDABLE BUT NOT CHEAP'. We were inundated with applications and ended up with the second-highest membership in the country after

Lancashire. The following year I was in the Caribbean with England before spending two more off-seasons in New Zealand, this time with Otago. My last stint was in 1997–98, after Glamorgan had won the championship title, and that was a mistake. As player–coach I revelled in the coaching side, but was too tired to offer much as a player.

Sue and I were also unhappy with the arrangements Otago had made for us on the housing and schooling fronts. Warren Lees, the cricket association's chief executive, made various promises over the telephone. When we arrived in New Zealand I stayed in Auckland, because I was captaining England in the Cricket Max tournament while Sue, Tom and our daughter Ceri flew on to Dunedin. We had expected to go back to the house we'd lived in the previous year – as Lees had promised us – but we ended up in a different area. I had wanted to tell Otago the previous July that I would not be coming, but Sue said I must honour my word even though I had not signed a contract. When we were told Ceri could not be enrolled in the local infants' school because she was too young, despite assurances from Lees that he would sort everything out, it was the last straw and I have remained at home every winter since.

I would encourage any young player to spend the winter playing abroad. Not only do you enjoy a double summer and keep fit, but experiencing different cultures and attitudes widens your perspective. I had always thought of New Zealand as a rugby country, just as outsiders do of Wales; but cricket was an important part of the sporting fabric, as it is in Wales, and it showed me how wrong preconceptions can be.

Not that staying at home means the putting up of feet. When I took over as captain of Glamorgan in 1996, I organised a series of fitness tests for players in the off-season. It seemed a good idea at the time – but I was not so sure on 1 November 2000, when I was the former Glamorgan captain undergoing bleep tests and the like. When I joined Glamorgan, pre-season fitness amounted to a three-mile run. If you did it in under 21 minutes you were fit; if you didn't, you were given a series of routines to do, but even if you were hungover and nursing a sore knee, you would have done it in the time.

I have also returned to work in the winter, planning for the day when I am no longer a professional cricketer. I am paid by Glamorgan over 11 months now, rather than 6. I got fed up of being in hock to the bank manager at the start of the season and the only month when I am not paid is October, because that is when any bonuses are paid, along with personal deals such as bat sponsorships.

My first bat deal was with Duncan Fearnley and was worth around £1,000 a year. You could have as many bats as you wanted and I went through three or four each season. I had used Gunn & Moore before Rodney Ontong introduced me to Duncan Fearnley and his bats were something else. When I went on the England tour I went over to Open Championship, who were offering £5,000 a year, but all I did was put their logos on Duncan's bats: he owed me a couple of bob and agreed to carry on making my sticks. The best bat I have had was the one with which I hit my century at Taunton in the match that decided the 1997 championship.

Two years ago I switched to Slazenger. Duncan had changed his bats and I was having trouble hitting the ball where I was aiming it. Slazenger had got hold of some excellent willow and their bats have been almost as good as the ones Duncan made in his heyday. For a time, I went along with the fashion for heavy bats – Ian Botham and Graham Gooch set that trend – but today I prefer lighter ones. Especially against the quicker bowlers, it is easier to hook with a light bat; a heavy bat is better to deal with the spinners, though, because a mis-hit is more likely to clear the field.

Cricket has given me a comfortable living, but I could have done better. During the 2000 one-day triangular tournament between England, Sri Lanka and West Indies, I was talking with Alec Stewart and Graeme Hick. Stewy was approaching his 100th England appearance and he was well into three figures for one-day internationals. Hick was coming up to his 60th cap and he, too, had played in more than 100 one-dayers. I had been capped before either of them, yet I had a mere four caps and had played in just a dozen one-dayers: the old man of the side, but not the most experienced.

Despite that, I do not feel that I have missed the boat. I was given my chance, if not an extended one, but I seem to have contrived unusual ways of getting out in an England sweater. The fatalist in me says that my England career was not to be. All the same, I still back myself against any bowling attack and think I had the ability to succeed at the highest level. Of course, I would say that, wouldn't I?

10. TRIUMPH

Glamorgan may not be the most fashionable of counties, but I don't believe that the reason I have not played for England more is that I was not with a bigger side. Glamorgan supporters have felt hard done by over the years and I certainly felt that Hugh Morris and Steve Watkin should have played many more times for England.

Hugh only won three England caps, even though he had qualities they were crying out for at the time: obduracy, consistency and dependability. He had dodgy knees by the end of his career, a legacy of an earlier rugby career, but they were in a better state than Mike Atherton's back. Watty was one of the best bowlers of his generation, nagging in length and clever in his variation. I would put him on a par with Angus Fraser, a typically British bowler with his ability to swing and seam the ball and get through any number of overs in a day.

Hugh and Watty were far more consistent than me and therefore have more cause to feel short changed on the international front. And Steve James, who took over as Glamorgan captain from me, has only won two caps despite a succession of remarkably prolific seasons. Like Hugh, he found his way blocked by Atherton, Alec Stewart and, at the start, Graham Gooch.

Our main problem was that Glamorgan were too often unsuccessful. England selectors seldom wasted their time watching struggling sides. But when we enjoyed a successful year, as we did in 1993, the story was different: that winter, Watty and I toured West Indies with England while Hugh, Robert Croft and Adrian Dale went abroad with England A (and Colin Metson was desperately unlucky to miss out). It is too easy to blame a bias among the selectors. We all had the chance to move elsewhere.

That is another reason why signing the right overseas player is important for a county. If he helps bring you success, this raises the profile of the other players as well as their standards and I do not think it was a coincidence that five of us were recognised by England at the end of Viv Richards's stay with us. It also reflected the emphasis that had been stressed by Alan Butcher: success is collective.

The summer of 1993 was the best of my career – not so much in terms of performance, though I did get back into the England side for the final two Tests against Australia, but because Glamorgan challenged for trophies on three fronts. We finished third in the championship, our best position for 24 years; we reached the semi-finals of the NatWest Trophy; and we won the Sunday League. Hugh had devised a game-plan which was simple but highly effective, based on aggression with the bat and containment with the ball.

We lacked a genuine fast bowler, but in Steve Watkin, Roland Lefebvre, Steve Barwick and Robert Croft, we had a quartet who between them only went for 2.5 runs an over. It made us a particularly effective one-day side, but it was also an approach which worked in the championship, where matches were all being played over four days for the first time with sides facing each other once in the season. The Sunday League had also been changed, to 50 overs from 40, and that worked to our advantage: our previous highest place in that competition (which started in 1969) had been fifth in 1988, one of only two seasons when we had finished in the top half of the table.

We went on a pre-season tour to South Africa, staying in Cape Town. We were playing Nottinghamshire in a one-day game and that night I went out for a meal which turned into an all-night drinking session. When Hugh Davies walked into breakfast at 7 a.m., he remarked that he was impressed to see me up so early, unaware that I'd not yet gone to bed. When I went out to bat later, Chris Lewis nearly took my head off with his first ball to me, a brutal bouncer. It sobered me up and I went on to hit 70. I have always been someone who has enjoyed a beer, but there is no way I would have stayed up all night had we been playing a first-class match.

I was Hugh's vice-captain in 1993 and, after we had played Oxford

University, our first match was against Kent in the Benson & Hedges Cup at Canterbury. When we had been in Cape Town we had held a brainstorming session with Paul Russell, of Andersen Consulting, and John Attenborough, a motivational expert. We based our strategy around beating Kent: they had been a bogey side to us in one-day cricket and Paul felt that if we beat them it would set us up for the season. When I asked him much later what would have happened to the plan had we lost at Canterbury, he just shrugged and said, 'God only knows.'

Kent were duly beaten by 104 runs. I won the gold award for hitting 89 in our 236 for 7 after Kent had put us into bat. The England coach, Keith Fletcher, was among the spectators and I was available for international cricket again after my ban – though at that stage I did not give my chances of a recall a second thought. Steve Barwick took 4 for 15 as we dismissed Kent for 132. Little did we know it then, but our season was to end at the same ground and with the same outcome.

Our championship campaign got off to a winning start as we defeated Sussex by 274 runs at Sophia Gardens. Five batsmen scored half-centuries, while Watty and Robert Croft did the damage with the ball, and we followed it up with a 191-run victory at Derbyshire: Hugh and I scored centuries and Watty picked up another five-wicket haul. We were on our way, and though Middlesex ended up winning the championship by 36 points, we had played no small part in their success.

There is something about Glamorgan and Middlesex. We have a dire record against them in the championship. When we won at Southgate in the 2000 season, it was our first success against them in the championship away from home for 42 years and there was something about them that brought out the worst in us. When we played them in Cardiff at the beginning of July in 1993, we knew it was a crucial match with both sides pushing for the title.

Hugh won the toss for that game and batted on an excellent wicket. We were 114 for 3 when Adrian Dale and Viv Richards came together. They put on an unbroken stand of 425 for the fourth wicket, both scoring double-centuries, in a record stand for any wicket for the county. They took our score to 562 for 3 before Hugh declared: some in the dressing-room felt that he should have carried on and put the game totally beyond Middlesex, but at the time I felt he was right because we needed the time to bowl them out twice.

John Emburey and Mike Gatting scored centuries for Middlesex. Gatt decided not to declare short of our total after passing the follow-on target and we eventually bowled them out for 584. A draw seemed the only outcome, but Phil Tufnell then took advantage of a turning wicket and turned in figures of 8 for 29 as we slumped to 109 all-out. That left Middlesex needing just 88 runs to win and they knocked them off without any trouble to leave us wondering how we had managed to conjure up a defeat out of a seemingly impregnable position.

We won our next three championship matches, but Middlesex had developed such a momentum that they proved impossible to catch and we had to concede defeat. Four years later, when we were chasing the title again, we again lost to Middlesex in humiliating fashion, but by then we were mentally stronger and could treat it as a one-off.

In August that year, at Neath, I scored 132 against the Australians, whose attack included Merv Hughes and Shane Warne. I reached my century off just 73 balls in a match which was televised live in Wales – or at least parts of it: when I was on 99, viewers were treated to a farming programme. I became the first player to hit 100 in a single session against Australia since Ian Botham in 1981 and it earned me my second cap after a clamour in the press.

Less than a week later I was facing the Aussies again, in the fifth Test at Edgbaston. The Ashes had already been lost, Australia having an unassailable 3–0 lead in the series with only two matches to go. Graham Gooch had resigned the captaincy after the failure, Mike Atherton taking over. And Watty had been named with me in the squad after enjoying another excellent season with the ball, but he ended up sitting out the match and played in the final Test.

I did not have much sleep the night before the first day. Nothing to do with staying up late or being afflicted by nerves, though. Sue gave birth to our daughter, Ceri, at 3.40 a.m. I marked the occasion by getting a duck after coming out to bat before lunch, brilliantly caught at silly point off the spinner Tim May. I was on a high after learning of Ceri's birth and my lack of sleep was in no way to blame for my failure.

I made ten in my second innings, given out caught behind off May, though I was convinced I'd not hit the ball. My bat hit my pad and the noise probably influenced the umpire. We lost by eight wickets and it marked a disappointing return for me, though I did have the consolation of receiving a huge bottle of bubbly after winning BBC Radio *Test Match Special*'s champagne moment for the run-out of Mark Taylor. Gooch was also presented with a bottle of champagne after passing David Gower to becoming the greatest run-scorer in England's history. His small bottle looked puny compared to mine, which hardly seemed right given the huge difference in our achievements – so I swapped with him. The England dressing-room was hardly bubbling and it contrasted unfavourably with Glamorgan's, but I was made to feel welcome by Mike Atherton and, going into the sixth Test, I felt I had something to offer at this level.

By then there was speculation about who would be going on the winter tour to West Indies and Warne let me know that my place was anything but a formality. I had made 20 in my first innings at the Oval and felt confident, coming down the wicket to Warne to hit him through mid-wicket. Then I left a delivery which pitched outside off stump, thinking it would turn away. I had misread him and the googly came back to hit my off stump. In the second innings, I fell into a leg trap and failed to keep the ball down when trying to hook Merv Hughes.

We won the game by 161 runs, with Watty playing a major part. He took six wickets in the match, four in Australia's second innings, and I took two catches off him. It was to be his last Test match, a fact I still struggle to understand. If it could be argued that I had done nothing with England to merit an extention to my international career, the same could not be said of Watty. He was treated badly, like a lot of other players from virtually every county.

We returned for the end of Glamorgan's Sunday League campaign. We had made a poor start in the tournament, losing narrowly at Derbyshire and against Northamptonshire at Pentyrch – my village club's first and only first-class match. We played one match every season in the Taff-Ely borough: sometimes it was a touring team, but more often it was a Sunday League game and Pontypridd had always been the venue. But there had been a bust-up between the Taff-Ely and Pontypridd councils after the Taff-Ely mayor was forced to walk through a park to the ground with rain in the air – despite his rather loud chain of office – because a jobsworth had refused to let his chauffeur park his car by the ground.

I knew how he felt. You had to have car-parking passes to get anywhere near the changing-rooms. In 1992 we played Derbyshire in Pontypridd. I had given my pass to Sue and just drove into the ground behind Viv Richards who was not one to worry about whether he had a pass. The guy at the gate stopped Viv and demanded to see his pass. I can imagine what Viv said, to the effect that the man did not know who he was. If there was a flicker of recognition, the jobsworth did not show it. We were decked out in red blazers in those days: perhaps he thought Viv was a bus driver, but there was no way he was going to let him in. I got out of the car to talk to the guy, but he wouldn't listen to someone else posing as a player. Where were all these red blazers coming from?

I pleaded and pleaded with him, but there was no way he was going to let us in. Eventually I lost patience with him and said that if the Glamorgan captain (I was leading the side in Alan Butcher's place) and our star player were not allowed in, there would be no match. The gateman eventually got on his two-way radio and, after being given orders he clearly did not agree with, reluctantly let us in. (Viv took out his anger on the Derbyshire attack by cracking a century before rain put an end to proceedings.)

But there was clearly no way that gateman was going to budge when it came to the mayor and Pontypridd lost their fixture for a year. Tony Dilloway, then Glamorgan's commercial manager, was in a panic when he found out that Pontypridd had been blacklisted by Taff-Ely, for there was no obvious alternative ground. The fixture was important to Glamorgan because the council offered the club a cash guarantee in return for a fixture. I mentioned the Pentyrch ground, which was only a six-hit from my house, and Tony returned relieved after inspecting the facilities.

The Pentyrch club enjoyed their 15 minutes of fame and there was little in the match on a slow wicket, Northamptonshire squeezing home with two balls to spare to win by three wickets – a defeat which put us on the bottom of the table. We got our first points when our game at Taunton the following week was washed out without a ball being bowled. Then we reeled off 12 consecutive victories, a streak which came to an end when rain in Cardiff washed out our match with Essex, just as we had them reeling at 7 for 2.

Our policy was to bat first if we won the toss, confident that we had the bowlers to constrict the opposition even if we were defending a small total: eight of the twelve victories came after we had had first knock. On the four occasions when we batted second, the largest total we had to chase was 208 and with bowlers like Roly Lefebvre, Steve Barwick, Watty and Robert Croft, no one took liberties with us. Anyway, we always had Viv and Adrian Dale as back-up. Hugh planned the campaign with military precision, operating his bowlers in pairs, and it worked before teams got used to it the following year.

The one time the plan backfired in 1993 was in the NatWest Trophy semi-final against Sussex at Hove. We were in sight of our first Lord's final for 16 years in what would have been a fitting way for Viv to end his career as a first-class cricketer. We had beaten Oxfordshire, Durham and Worcestershire comfortably on our way to the last four and we were favourites to defeat Sussex, even though they had dumped us out of the Benson & Hedges Cup in Cardiff.

I hit 84 to take my season's aggregate in the NatWest to 336 runs, but we felt that our final score of 220 was at least 20 runs too short. Not that we thought we would lose, because we'd won several one-day matches that year in similar positions and we soon had Sussex in trouble. It was only in the 18th over that the scoreboard showed more runs than overs and at 110 for 6 they were in trouble. Our seamers had bowled superbly, with Watty, Roly and Baz all hard to get away and Adrian Dale taking two vital wickets. Roly's incredible catching had been a feature of our season and he was at it again at Hove, catching Martin Speight off Watty.

Sussex needed eight an over with their last two recognised batsmen at the wicket, Alan Wells and Neil Lenham. Wells batted superbly, ending unbeaten on 106, but he was actually run out by Viv halfway through his innings. The umpire, Kenny Palmer, gave Wells the benefit of the doubt, but television replays showed he had been out of his ground when the ball hit the stumps. Third umpires were in those days used only in one-day finals, but the furore after that Wells decision led to technology subsequently being used at every match where live television coverage was taking place. Kenny gave that one as he saw it, though, which was fair enough: there wasn't a lot in it and he had to give the batsman the benefit of any doubt.

We lost it because Viv and Crofty went for 77 runs in their 12 overs between them, with Wells and Lenham going on the attack against them. We failed to respond quickly enough and lost by three wickets with just four balls remaining – only a couple of tight overs away from Lord's and it was bitterly disappointing to have lost a match which at one stage we appeared to have in the bag.

What was important was that it did not affect our push for the Sunday League. Four days later we found ourselves defending a similar total at Leicester after scoring 228 for 7. James Whitaker scored a century, but we held on to win by eight runs and were back on course. It all boiled down to the final match of the season against the leaders Kent at Canterbury: winner would take all and, like us, they had only lost two matches all season. We hoped to win the toss and bat, but Hugh called wrongly and Kent decided to set us a target.

At one stage, with Carl Hooper and Matthew Fleming in full flow, we looked like having to chase more than 250 runs, but Baz and Crofty applied the brakes and Kent finished on 200 for 9. With a large and noisy Welsh contingent at the ground, we were confident of getting the runs and found ourselves well placed at 84 for 1 with Hugh and Adrian 'Arthur Daley' Dale cruising. But Arthur went, quickly followed by myself, and when Hugh was dismissed for 67 to leave us at 141 for 4, the match was in the balance.

It was the perfect stage for Viv who, with Tony Cottey, took us home with 14 balls to spare and there were scenes of noisy and unrestrained joy. After we had been presented with the trophy, Glamorgan secretary Mike Fatkin took a firm hold of it and said the cup was not going to disappear from his sight that night. As he went down the pavilion steps, he passed a man who remarked what a wonderful trophy it was.

'I wouldn't care if it was a piece of wood covered in dog's mess,' replied Mike. 'It's ours.'

And off he stomped, not realising that he had been talking to the chief executive of AXA Equity and Law, the sponsors of the Sunday League.

11. FAILURE

I was sitting up in bed looking at a knuckle that I suspected was broken and wondering if I had wrecked my career as a first-class cricketer. It was May 1994 and the celebrations at Canterbury seemed a different world away. The previous night I had punched a man in a Cardiff street and left him on the ground, fleeing the scene like a fugitive. I was too afraid to read the newspapers and, even though the England squad was due to be announced shortly, I was afraid of the telephone ringing or of someone knocking at the door. Everything was falling apart.

It had all looked so different the previous autumn as I trained at Lilleshall with the England squad in preparation for the West Indies tour. We went to Portugal for some warm-weather work and I scored a century in a training match. We let our hair down at the end of our week there, and even Jack Russell ended up the worse for wear. He hardly touched a drop of alcohol and it did not take much to put him away. Devon Malcolm and I carried him to bed.

I made the headlines for the wrong reasons shortly before we left for the Caribbean. I went to a pub near Pentyrch to wet my daughter Ceri's head. There were 20 of us in the pub – including Steve Gough, the golf professional at the Radyr club in Cardiff, and Glamorgan secretary Mike Fatkin, whose respective wives had also just given birth – and we'd organised a pool tournament with the proceeds going to charity. The beer flowed and I brought a couple of friends back to the house with me. They lived in Cardiff and at about 2 a.m. I telephoned for a taxi. It failed to turn up so I called again, to be told it would be with us in five minutes. Half an hour went by and it was clear that the cab was not going to turn up.

Stupidly, I offered the guys a lift. On the way into Cardiff, I pulled up at a red light. I was in a sponsored Mercedes with the sun-roof open and the stereo blaring. I could not have been more conspicuous had I walked to the wicket without a stitch of clothing on. A policeman sitting in his car heard the racket and pulled me over. I asked him why he had stopped me and received the reply that I had skidded before braking at the lights. The car had ABS, so I knew that could not be true, but he hardly had to ask if I had been drinking. I was more than three times over the limit and I spent the night in a cell, eventually getting fined £500 and being banned from driving for 18 months.

I deserved everything I got and it could have happened earlier. I had often driven home after a day's play having downed three or four pints of beer. I felt not only embarrassed but ashamed. I had let down Sue, my family and the Glamorgan club. My shame was a public one because my court hearing was, rightly, reported in the media. The only silver lining for me was that I had not committed the offence during daylight hours when there would have been more traffic on the road and children on the pavements. It was a great lesson for me, and since then I have never had more than a couple of weak shandies if I am going to get behind the wheel.

It meant that for the following season, I was going to have to beg for lifts, and I was off the beaten track in Pentyrch. At least the only driving I had to worry about in the Caribbean was when I had a bat in my hand – but with the likes of Curtly Ambrose and Courtney Walsh in the West Indies line-up, there were not going to be many invitations to get onto the front foot.

We trained in the autumn for what we were going to get in the Test matches: unremittingly hostile fast bowling. Viv Richards may have retired from Test cricket and the West Indies were starting a slow decline, but they were still one of the best sides in the world, while England were nowhere near the first division. We got off the plane in Antigua and as I was walking down the steps, I heard the clanking of bottles. Robin Smith staggered onto the tarmac and walked towards the bus that was going to take us to our hotel as if he were a skier on a slalom course. On the coach he shouted abuse to passing locals, saying we were England and we were out there to win. He became a very good friend of mine and as my tour degenerated he kept me from going completely off the rails.

There is no better place to go on a cricket tour than the islands which make up the West Indies. Everywhere we went the locals had a passionate interest in cricket, which extended far beyond facts and figures. You would be walking in the street or sitting at a bar and someone would come up to you and ask why you played this or that shot the previous day, why you didn't play the ball through a certain area more, or, if you were a bowler, why you didn't have this or that field setting. Their love of the game shone through and they were never abusive. 'Maynard, I've seen you bat, man. Like your style, aggressive like a West Indian' – that was a remark I heard more than once. They were not so keen on stonewallers, though.

I took interacting with the locals a little too far in the final match of the best-of-five one-day series that tour. We were playing in Trinidad and coming to the end of the West Indian innings. It was hot and the drinks break had long gone. I licked my lips after a 40-yard run from long-on to deep extra cover to stop a boundary and someone in the crowd, taking pity on me, offered me his cola. I took a grateful swig but, the next moment, Roger Harper hit Angus Fraser straight to where I was standing. My fielding in the series had been excellent, better than my batting, and it was a regulation catch. Yet it went straight through my hands and as I looked for a hole to open up in front of me, the crowd went mad; when I looked round there were dozens of coke bottles being waved at me.

The next over saw me positioned at deep extra. The ball came skimming towards me and, as I went down to pick it up, it reared off a divot and I had to move my head smartly out of the way: four runs and more bottle waving. Shortly afterwards I dropped Harper off Gus again and the crowd were in full voice – far better entertainment than the cricket itself. Gus said nothing to me, which was a surprise because he hated incompetent fielding off his bowling, but during the tea interval he threw a bread roll at me.

The itinerary was staggered, with the opening one-day international followed by the first Test. The other four one-dayers were then played en bloc and we were left with just two more first-class matches outside the other four Tests. I shared a room with Phil Tufnell a lot, since we both smoked, and got to know a different side of him. I also roomed with Chris Lewis for a while. He was a different character to Tuffers, sometimes misunderstood. He liked to do things for effect, such as shaving his head shortly after we had arrived in the Caribbean (and going down with the sunstroke he had thought he was immune to because of his dark skin).

The harsh reality of what lay in store for us came in the first of two friendlies. We were cruising against Antigua, with both Mike Atherton and Alec Stewart scoring centuries, only to lose a flurry of wickets. I played in the next match against St Kitts and Nevis, dismissed for two: 'Maynard lbw Maynard,' the scorecard read. I had been dismissed by John Maynard, who was known to the locals as the Dentist, for his fiery fast bowling had rearranged the teeth of several batsmen. One of my rivals for a place in the Test side, Mark Ramprakash, scored 136 while another, Nasser Hussain, was out for a duck.

Our opening first-class match was against the Leeward Islands. I made 25 in a match we won comfortably and sat out the final game before the opening Test against Barbados. It ended in a draw after Barbados's opening bowler had taken 5 for 87. I would come across Ottis Gibson again when he joined Glamorgan later in the year. I had no idea whether I would keep my place in the Test side: being the man in possession seemed to tilt it my way.

The first day of the first Test started well for us. Atherton and Stewart put on 121 for the first wicket, but you could never relax against West Indies then because they had a battery of fast bowlers rather than just two. By the close of play we were 209 for 7. I was unbeaten on 24, already the third-highest scorer in the innings, batting with Andy Caddick with just Alan Igglesden and Devon Malcolm to come.

When Caddick went at the beginning of the second day, I decided to get on with it and was ninth out at 227 with 35. We made 234, a total West Indies passed quickly on their way to 407. We improved, marginally, in the second innings – though I got my second duck for England – and after scoring 267, the West Indies' victory target was a mere 95. One surprise was that they softened up Devon Malcolm, our last batsman. Dev was a genuine number 11 and I could not work out why Walsh kept peppering him with short-pitched deliveries, several of which struck Dev in the ribs and on his arms. It must have been their strategy: we barely had a chance of winning, our only hope being Dev firing on all cylinders, and his ordeal at the crease took the fire out of him.

I played in the rest of the one-dayers. West Indies took the series 3–2, winning the middle three matches. The low point came at St Vincent where Mike Atherton was conned by a couple of locals into putting West Indies in if he won the toss. They claimed that the wicket got easier as a match went on, but the opposite was true, as we were to find out. They made 313 for 6 in 50 overs, which was then a record score in a one-day international. Desmond Haynes and Brian Lara led the way before Richie Richardson smote 52 off just 26 deliveries. The pitch got slower and lower and was by the end virtually dead, with balls shooting along the ground. Our 148 for 9 was still a poor response, but so was the reaction of Keith Fletcher.

He lost the confidence of a number of players when he ranted and raved instead of analysing what had gone wrong. Fletcher seemed to sum up the hope-rather-than-expectation approach which infected the national set-up at that time. He could see things slipping away and clearly realised that there was nothing he could do about it. He was the wrong man in the wrong place.

After the one-day series had finished my tour was virtually over. We played a West Indies Board XI in Guyana. Graham Thorpe and Mark Ramprakash put on 158 for the second wicket, with Ramps finishing unbeaten on 154. I added an unbroken 106 with him for the third wicket, but my 40 not out did not compare with his knock and he played in the remaining four Test matches. In one sense I could not argue, but I thought I deserved another chance after Kingston. You need time to adjust to Test cricket, but my time seemed to be up.

I played just one more match, that miserable game against a Board XI in Grenada when Fletcher refused to let me go in as nightwatchman. He may as well have told me to catch the next plane home: his defeatist attitude had become infectious and it was only when the series had been lost, West Indies winning the second and third Tests comfortably, that we became competitive. Alec Stewart scored a century in each innings in Barbados to lead the way to a 208-run victory. Gus took eight wickets in the first innings, with Andy Caddick claiming five in the second. Steve Watkin, who five years later was to become my brother-in-law after marrying Sue's sister, Caryl, did not get a look-in all series – ignored because conditions in West Indies were not seen to favour seam bowlers, so why was he taken in the first place? Personally, I would back Watty in any conditions.

The last Test in Antigua was a draw which has gone down in history because Brian Lara hit 375 to break Sir Gary Sobers's record for the highest individual score in a Test match. Lara seemed destined then to follow in Viv Richards's footsteps at the very least and he suddenly became the hottest property in the game. Unfortunately for him, West Indies were about to pay for not investing heavily enough in the development of their cricket at the time when they were pre-eminent in the world – much like Welsh rugby in the 1970s – and as they rejoined the ranks of the mortals on the way to levelling out with England, Lara struggled to cope with the pressure of being their only world-class batsman. His Test batting average is still better than most, but he has not achieved what everyone said he would during that April day in Antigua.

I started the tour knowing that it was my chance to establish my place in the England side for the next couple of years, but I finished it feeling like Keith Fletcher's slave and it took me a long time to get over the knock to my self-esteem. Far too long. I wish I had been tougher inside and given Fletcher a piece of my mind. It wasn't long before he was on his way back to Essex, an environment he is clearly happier in and where he has achieved a lot: he just did not have the temperament to be a national coach, especially when he was in charge of a side which was struggling.

I returned home that April and in less than a week found myself playing for Glamorgan against Warwickshire at Edgbaston. As I was unable to drive, I got lifts everywhere and it meant that I drank more, especially when I was staying in hotels with temptation on tap. Steve Barwick kept me company as I cursed the injustice of it all while Watty, who had more to complain about than me, carried on taking wickets.

My form at the start of the 1994 season was dreadful. I made 55 runs in four championship innings and desperately wanted a break from the game. I did get a break – though not in the manner I had sought. I'd been to one of Hugh Morris's Benefit events in Cardiff, a lunch which had gone on far longer than I had expected. I was walking down

Westgate Street when some guy I had never seen before started accosting me. He kept jabbing his finger in my chest and asked who I thought I was, strutting around when Glamorgan were doing so badly: I couldn't score a run, I was no use and so on, a torrent of invective. I had become used to dealing with spectators criticising things I had done, but usually I was able to discuss things in a rational manner.

Rational was a word this bloke did not understand. As he kept going on at me, he became more aggressive and threatening. I could not get away from him and I felt threatened. I hadn't had that much to drink and, anyway, the effect alcohol has on me is to make me happy, not aggressive. However, I decided to get my retaliation in first and caught him with a right hook. He fell to the floor and I did not hang around to see what happened next. I had never been involved in a violent incident like that before and could not believe what I had done.

When I got home, it became clear that my knuckle was in a bad way. I was meant to be leading Glamorgan in a one-day Second XI match at Worcester the following day. The firsts were not in action and it was felt that I needed time in the middle when what should have been obvious to everyone was that I needed to get away from cricket for a while. Tony Cottey drove me to Worcester and I told him what had happened the previous night.

I expected the guy I'd punched to go to the police. I worried that once what I had done became public, my hopes of ever playing again for England would be dashed and Glamorgan might even reconsider my future with them. I was in turmoil and it just seemed that one bad thing was following another. There was no way I could tell the club why I had a broken knuckle. Fortunately, as I warmed up at Worcester, a ball rapped me on the glove and that gave me the excuse I needed. I batted and took a couple of catches when we fielded, but once the X-ray had revealed a break, I had the three weeks off that I craved.

I still dreaded reading a newspaper, for fear the man whom I'd hit would have told all, but he must have been so much the worse for wear that the following morning he could not remember what had happened to him. It is something I have never forgotten and I can still see his face now.

What I did was inexcusable and totally out of character. If it had happened the previous year I don't think there is any way that I would have hit him; but I was mentally a wreck after all that had happened over the previous eight months, to the extent that something inside me snapped. I still find the knowledge of what I did frightening and in my three weeks off I reflected what I was: a drink-driver who went around hitting people in the street. It was time I sorted myself out.

I returned to action against Derbyshire in the middle of June and scored 118, my only championship century of the season, though I did take 101 off the South Africans at Pontypridd. I ended up keeping wicket briefly during the match when Adrian Shaw was taken to hospital after being hit in the mouth and picked up the third first-class stumping of my career: Hansie Cronje off Robert Croft for 78.

I just missed out on 1,000 runs and my average of 36.11 meant I was nowhere near getting back into the England squad. More than that, Glamorgan had had a dreadful season. We finished bottom of the championship – something I thought we had put behind us – marooned at the foot of the table 32 points behind Derbyshire, the side I could have been with that year. We did better in the Sunday League, finishing seventh, but we would have been second if we'd not lost two of our three final matches. We fell at the first hurdle in the Benson & Hedges Cup, losing against Surrey at The Oval. Surrey also ended our interest in the NatWest Trophy, comfortable winners at St Helen's.

One season of triumph, the most successful in Glamorgan's history, had been followed by one of our worst. My personal life reflected the side's – 1994 was my *annus horribilis* – but it was just as Kipling said: you have to treat the twin impostors exactly the same. It's only when you have endured the lows that you can really appreciate the highs and I realised that our success in 1993 had not been an end. It was just a beginning. I became fired by the ambition to lead Glamorgan and I was not too sure how long Hugh would want to continue in charge. Like me, he had fallen short of 1,000 runs in 1994 and it was unlike him to miss out on the landmark. It is in adversity that you find your true self.

LEFT: Liverpool Arms, 1977. With Charlie (left), Mum and Dad.

BELOW: Rodney Marsh? More like Rodney Trotter, but from the age of four I have remained a true Sky Blue.

ABOVE: Never one to blow my own trumpet! Charlie and I empty the public bar of the Liverpool Arms.

RIGHT: Wedding day. With Sue at Menai Bridge at the end of 1996.

ABOVE: A sponsored car to remember.
My wheels in New Zealand in 1987 –
shame about the spelling.

RIGHT: The night before. Steve Gough
and I hold our new-born daughters
before going to celebrate their arrivals
– to excess, as it turned out. I was
banned from driving for 18 months
after failing a breath-test.

BELOW: Family portrait. With Sue,
Tom and Ceri.

Shell Trophy success. Celebrating with Northern Districts in New Zealand in 1991 – seven Kiwi internationals present and future were in the side.

The mighty daffodil. My son Tom helps launch our 1993 membership drive with (clockwise from top left) Terry Yorath, then the Wales soccer manager; Ieuan Evans, the Wales rugby captain; television presenter Sara Edwards; and comedian Owen Money.
© Huw John

Edgbaston,1993. With my mentor, Bill Clutterbuck, before the fifth Test against Australia.
© Huw John

ABOVE: Some like it hot. On Bird Island in 1994 with Robin Smith, Viv Richards and our ship's captain, Eric, after a successful fishing trip in the Caribbean.

BELOW: Corks out. Steve Watkin and I celebrate our call-up into the England squad during the 1993 Ashes series. Watty became my brother-in-law in 1999 when he married Sue's sister, Caryl. © Huw John

LEFT: One hand on the trophy. Sweeping a four to beat Essex in the penultimate game of the 1997 championship, one victory away from the title. © Huw John

BELOW: Gloves on. Wicket-keeping against Durham in the National League in 1999. Paul Collingwood is the striker. © Huw John

ABOVE: Eat your heart out, Courtney Walsh. Umpire Alan Whitehead looks on in admiration at the pie-thrower from Pentyrch! © Huw John

BELOW: Party time. The beginning of a long night at Taunton after our first championship title for 28 years. Tom is on the right of the picture with a fizzy drink! © Huw John

Close shave. Setting a trend long before David Beckham after a mishap with my beard trimmer in Otago in 1997. © Huw John

Up she goes. Playing Shane Warne with both hands on the bat is difficult enough. Fortunately, I got away with it against Hampshire in 2000. Wicket-keeper Adrian Aymes looks on. © Huw John

ABOVE: Lord's here we come. Tuning up for the Glamorgan song after beating Surrey in the 2000 Benson & Hedges Cup semi-final. Wordsmith Owen Parkin is pictured front left. © Huw John

BELOW: The smile says it all. Celebrating our 1997 championship success. © Huw John

12. ALL BETS ARE OFF

Cricket to me is about small margins: a faint edge which the umpire may or may not pick up; a slight adjustment in the field which sometimes works and on other occasions makes you look a fool; a premeditated decision to play a certain shot which has the capacity to backfire if the bowler reads your intentions; and getting the timing of a declaration right. Cricket is a complicated game in terms of its laws. There are pages of them, not always written in the clearest of language, but the essence of the sport, like any other, is simple – win.

At the end of the 1999 campaign, the South Africa captain Hansie Cronje agreed to succeed Duncan Fletcher as the coach of Glamorgan. It was another big coup for us: signing someone of Hansie's stature, having lost Duncan to England, was not only good for our image but it would also mean we were replacing quality with quality. No longer was Glamorgan a side content to accept second best.

It was Fletch who suggested Cronje and when he first mentioned the name I didn't think we had a prayer, even though Hansie had once spent a season with Leicestershire. He was the captain of his country and South Africa had ambitions of overhauling Australia at the top of the world table. Even Fletch thought it was a long shot, but he felt it was worth giving it a go and we asked Jacques Kallis – our South African overseas player that year – to establish contact with Cronje for us.

Cronje had the reputation of an honest, committed cricketer who was respected the world over and he told Jacques he would be interested in joining us. He fancied a break from playing cricket and, it emerged, there had been a split at the top of South African cricket with Cronje coming under attack from certain selectors. He had not been reappointed for the series against England that winter, merely named as captain for the first two Tests. He felt vulnerable and we offered him a way out.

We offered him a two-year deal which would have meant him working nine months of each year in Wales. He signed the contract and faxed it over to Glamorgan secretary Mike Fatkin. We looked forward to him arriving in Wales at the end of January 2000 and celebrated our triumph. Having experienced South Africa at first hand, I should have known better than to take anything for granted. Within a few weeks of the club announcing that Cronje would succeed Fletch, Hansie asked if we would let him change his mind.

Ali Bacher, the man who had organised the 1989 'rebel' tour and who was now the head of South Africa's cricket board, had got to work on Hansie and reassured him about his future. The South African government also became involved and Cronje's critics on the selection panel found themselves isolated. The upshot was that he no longer wanted to commit himself to joining Glamorgan in 2000, though did say he would be interested in coaching us when he retired from international cricket.

We could have held him to the agreement he had signed, but there was no point. We wanted someone who was totally committed to the club – particularly as we were starting life in the new championship in the second division – and Hansie would clearly have had his mind elsewhere. We agreed to let him go. Six months later it was Hansie Cronje who was bitterly regretting that he had not come to Wales. He had found himself snared in a betting scandal which rocked the world game. He admitted taking bribes to fix matches and was eventually banned from the game for life. Had he come to Glamorgan, the chances are that nothing would have come to light because most of the charges which hooked him referred to matches played after we had released him from his contract.

Mike Fatkin was telephoned by one journalist after the affair had blown up and asked whether we would have appointed Hansie as coach had we known that he was a corrupt player who was on the take from bookmakers. Mike could barely disguise his incredulity at such a stupid question. Of all the players in the game, virtually the last one you would have suspected of being prepared to fix matches in return for a few dollars was God-fearing Hansie Cronje. It shows how wrong you can be. Small margins again.

I was in South Africa that winter, leading a touring party for the sports travel agency Gullivers. The final Test, uniquely in Test cricket, saw a contrived double-declaration to ensure a finish after South Africa had secured the series. England won a thrilling match, but when Cronje was indicted on various counts of match-fixing, there were suggestions that the victory was worthless because Hansie had arranged it that South Africa would lose.

Suddenly, every unlikely victory in cricket was thrown into question. I spoke to Hansie during that Test in Pretoria when the rain had threatened to turn it into a tame draw. He asked me what would have happened in the championship and I said that, more than likely, the two captains would have reached an agreement about a fourth-innings chase. He just nodded and there was then a suggestion that the South Africa board, anxious to attract a crowd when play did eventually resume, had offered its players a one-million-rand bonus if they won the Test. I remain convinced that England's victory, if unusual, was legitimate.

Cronje's deeds, and those of some others in Test cricket in the 1990s, means that no one will ever know for sure and suddenly all sorts of allegations were made. Chris Lewis, the former England all-rounder, made a statement implicating three of his former team-mates in a betting scandal without naming them. The England and Wales Cricket Board interviewed Lewis, but his evidence was never made public, which means that everyone who ever played international cricket with him remains tainted. Lewis was dismissed as an attention-seeker and he did not follow through with his allegations; but suddenly smoke started to billow.

My Glamorgan team-mate, Robert Croft, admitted that when he had been on tour with England in Sharjah he had received a telephone call from someone asking for information. He immediately put the phone down and told the management. When England were on tour in Pakistan at the end of 2000, an Indian bookmaker claimed he had given Alec Stewart £5,000 in 1993 for providing information about the

England side. Stewart, like Cronje, was a model cricketer whom you would never have suspected of being involved in something untoward, but he found himself in an invidious position because the onus was on him to prove his innocence. I couldn't begin to count the times that I have been asked before matches by spectators what I intend to do if I win the toss or who is going to be left out of the 12. And you pose for pictures with people you do not know. It is easy to set a cricketer up, but much more difficult for him to prove he has done something in all innocence rather than for any financial reward.

While the betting cloud hangs over Test cricket, I have never been asked to throw a county match, nor in my time as captain did an opposing skipper ever make what I felt was an over-generous declaration offer. There have been a couple of allegations, but they did not stand up to official scrutiny. I am not a gambler and if anyone had made overtures to me, I would have told them where to get off. That is not to say categorically there is not a problem – merely that if there is, I do not know anything about it.

There was one match when some Glamorgan players did have a bet – Kent in the Benson & Hedges Cup at Canterbury in 1993, the match we had targeted as being the key to our season. A few of the boys were wandering around the boundary when they saw a bookmaker's van. We were being quoted at odds of 7–2 to win and, in a two-horse race, it was a tempting flutter. They put a few quid on us and thought no more about it until the end of the match.

I don't have a problem with players betting on their own team to win, though that is now forbidden by the England and Wales Cricket Board – understandably, because there is an inherent danger of striking a deal with the opposition. And there is the growing menace of spread betting. I spoke to a rugby player a couple of years ago who said that his team-mates often placed money on their (English) team to lose: not on the pitch, but on the spread-betting sheet. If their opponents were given a 30-point start and lost by 25, it would be seen as a victory by the bookies. So you could win and still cash in for losing.

At the start of the 1997 season, I received a telephone call from a friend of mine in Hong Kong who advised me to take a spread bet on the Kent off-spinner Min Patel. The spread was that he would take between 50 and 60 wickets that season. Anything under or over that would be worth £100 a wicket. I was advised to go for less than 50 because Min had damaged his knee playing for the MCC that winter and the chances were that he would hardly play any championship cricket. In the event he only bowled three overs, without taking a wicket, before breaking down. I would have made £5,000, but to me the whole thing stank and I didn't put any money on.

Would it have been wrong, morally or otherwise, had I had a flutter, profiting from insider information? To me it was a form of cheating and that is something I have taken a strong line against on the field. I would guess that at the time I started my career, some 70 per cent of batsmen would walk if they'd edged the ball rather than wait for the umpire to give his verdict. That figure is now closer to seven per cent and, where I used to walk, I will now wait.

I got fed up with seeing batsmen who had clearly hit the ball staying at the crease and being given not out. If that happens, and someone goes on to score 50 or 100, I will not applaud. It is a strange ritual anyway, clapping someone who has tucked into your bowling with relish – a tradition which has had its day except when you have witnessed batting that is truly remarkable. You don't see the batsman at the non-striking end clap when a bowler takes his fifth wicket or a hat-trick. And why should he? He would be applauding the failure of his own side.

There are times when you're unsure whether you have got a nick, or whether the ball has been gathered cleanly, though I will still walk if I feel that the contact has been obvious. There are times when you are given out caught and you know only too well that you have not hit the ball; or that you have hit it, in the case of an lbw decision. Over the course of a season or a career, things balance themselves out. Umpires, like players, make mistakes and I think the sport has been right to make greater use of technology over the years. The third umpire was a welcome innovation.

But then there is not walking, and blatant cheating. We played a championship match against Leicestershire in 1994 and I hit a ball which Adrian Pierson picked up at mid-wicket off the bowling of Gordon Parsons on the half-volley. He had his eyes closed at the moment of fielding the ball and claimed the catch. I stood where I was, convinced that I was not out. The umpire, Vanburn Holder, gave me out without referring the incident to his fellow umpire David Constant at square leg. I had to go.

At the close of play I stormed into the Leicestershire dressing-room. I was angry not so much with Pierson – who probably was not sure whether it was a catch or not – but with their captain, Nigel Briers, who'd had a good view from his position in the field. I said that was not the way I'd want to win a match. Briers claimed he had been unsighted by the umpire. I got my revenge in their final innings when I caught Briers, legitimately, off Steve Watkin as we cruised to a 150-run victory. Leicestershire, under the captaincy of James Whitaker, were to take the championship title in 1996.

There was a similar incident when we played Hampshire in Southampton in the 1997 NatWest Trophy. We had to chase 303 to win – something we had never achieved in the competition – and we were going well when Steve James hit Shaun Udal to mid-wicket. He set off for a single, only to send Adrian Shaw back. Shaw had not made his ground when Udal took the bails off. Adrian trudged slowly off, having been given out, but he was convinced that Udal had broken the stumps without having the ball in his hand. 'Sid' James was furious and had a go at the Hampshire captain, John Stephenson, pointing his finger in uncharacteristically strident fashion. Matthew Hayden (the Australian international who had thrown in the ball to Udal) and Robin Smith asked the bowler if he had had the ball in his hands when he took the bails off. Udal said no.

Stephenson's attitude was 'so what?' – Shaw had been given out and Hampshire were one wicket closer to victory. Umpire Ray Julian overheard the conversation and intervened. When Udal confessed that he hadn't had the ball in his hands at the crucial moment, Julian called Shaw back.

Adrian had walked so slowly from the field that he was still a couple of yards from the point of no return, the boundary rope. Had he crossed it he would have been out, but as it was he could take his reprieve and went on to make an unbeaten 34 as we got home by two wickets with two balls left.

As a captain you have to play it straight. In my first year as the captain of Glamorgan in 1996, the players were annoyed after I had set Hampshire what they thought was an easy target at Southampton: 331

off a minimum of 96 overs. They feared that my friendship with the Hampshire captain, Robin Smith, had influenced my decision, but that was not the way I operated. I felt that our only chance of victory lay in setting Hampshire a total they felt they could reach. In the end, they were hanging on for a draw and the Glamorgan players had more respect for me after that.

But say we had lost. Questions could have been asked about my motives, whether based on friendship or something worse. That is the stain which will be left on the game by the betting scandals which blew up in the 1990s. Will anything be accepted at face value? When Glamorgan played Lancashire in the 1997 championship, I set them 273 off 60 overs after two days and two innings had been washed out. There were murmurings in the dressing-room that it was too generous and that I had been taken for a ride by my opposite number, Neil Fairbrother. It was a defining moment in our campaign that year: we had suffered a humiliating defeat against Middlesex in our previous match and we had to bounce back with a victory. I wasn't interested in a draw and that meant giving Lancashire hope.

I told the players that if anyone thought that the declaration was soft and that we had little chance of winning, I did not want them on the field – that I would rather go out with seven or eight other players who were confident about our chances, rather than be weighed down by two or three who were going to be groaning and moaning. In the event we rolled Lancashire over for 51 and our championship bid was back on track.

Bizarre situations occur in all sports. In my first year with Glamorgan, we played Nottinghamshire in a Sunday League match at Swansea and they needed 37 off the final two overs. Rodney Ontong took off Mark Price, who had been bowling well, and brought back the openers. We lost. A few years later we played Kent at Llanelli. They needed 51 off the final three overs and Steve Watkin was bowling. He was flayed everywhere and Kent won with a couple of balls to spare, the most unlikely of victories. 'It was like bowling on the highlights,' said a downcast Watty, memorably. It was an amazing finale by Kent, but today, I suppose, questions would be asked.

The England and Wales Cricket Board have now taken action so that any suspect finishes are now quickly investigated, but with spread betting the issue is very difficult to police. There was a soccer match a couple of years ago where a team kicked off and booted the ball into touch just to win a spread bet about when the first throw-in would be. No one was ever going to ask me to make a low score for England – the chances were that I would have made one without the need for any inducement – but pity the prolific batsman today who suffers an unexpected low score, particularly if playing a rash shot.

If I had been told during my time as the Glamorgan captain that one of my players had placed a bet against the side, he would have been suspended on the spot and I would never have picked him again. There would have been no extenuating circumstances, because he would have been violating one of the cardinal principles of sport: the need for trust between a team and its supporters, the wage payers.

What Hansie Cronje did was wrong and his life ban was the proper course of action by the South African board. Had he kept to his word and come to Glamorgan he would, I suspect, have survived with his reputation and his career in the sport intact and I have no doubt that he would not have tried anything on the gambling front with us. A coach is hardly in a position to solicit favours, because he does not pick the side and he does not play. Any word to a player to throw his wicket or bowl badly would soon get round the dressing-room.

Cronje did not just do himself a grievous disservice but also cricket itself. It is easy for someone to make allegations about players taking money to fix matches or give their wickets away: how do you prove that you *did no such thing*? The game has been tarnished and it will take years for it to recover.

13. TAKING A LEAD

By the end of the 1995 campaign Hugh Morris decided, for the second time, to give up the Glamorgan captaincy. His form was not the problem, as it had been in 1989: he scored a century in each innings in his last full match in charge against Nottinghamshire at Sophia Gardens, topped our batting averages and hit six centuries.

No, he went after having one run-in too many with the committee. The crunch came towards the end of the season when he dropped the wicket-keeper Colin Metson for the championship match against Gloucestershire at Abergavenny, though he softened the blow by saying that Adrian Shaw had been brought in because Metto was injured. He soon found himself answering to Hugh Davies, the chairman of the cricket committee.

Metto was in those days the selectorial equivalent of a sacred cow. He was highly regarded as a wicket-keeper, and rightly so, but he was more popular with the supporters and the committee than he was with the players in the dressing-room. We had not had a good season in 1995 in the championship, missing out on bottom place by beating Nottinghamshire, and we had lost three consecutive matches before Abergavenny. Hugh Morris felt that something needed to be done.

Hugh saw, as I was to see later, that Adrian Shaw offered different virtues to Metto, ones that a captain holds dear. But Hugh Davies wanted an explanation when he should have been publicly supporting Hugh's decision, whatever his private views. It highlighted, yet again, the problem in trying to run a professional team when there was constant interference from the committee rooms. Ironically, Hugh had been appointed captain ahead of me because he had been seen as the safer pair of hands; but the committee failed to appreciate that it doesn't matter what type of captain they appoint in terms of character and demeanour, whoever it is will look to do the job on his own terms and without interference.

That game against Gloucestershire was the most absorbing of our campaign on the small but picturesque ground at Abergavenny. The Australian Andrew Symonds scored an unbeaten 254 – an innings which contained a world-record 16 sixes – and the Indian fast bowler Javagal Srinath took 9 for 76, a remarkable return on a wicket renowned for breaking the hearts of the quicker bowlers. David Hemp and I put on 306 for the third wicket in Glamorgan's second innings, only seven runs short of the club record, but we slid from 424 for 2 to 471 all out.

Gloucestershire needed 325 to win, but the rain slowed them down and they crashed from 204 for 3 to 277 for 9, Darren Thomas whipping up a fair amount of pace. The last ball of the match was just out of reach of Alistair Dalton at short leg and a remarkable game of cricket ended in a draw. But the talk in the corridors of power was about Colin Metson, who was reinstated for the final three matches of the season. It was too much for Hugh, who, when he announced his decision to stand down, said pointedly that he had not enjoyed total support and that one or two in the club had tried to undermine his position.

Hugh tended to keep things to himself, so no one really knew what he was thinking, but the fact that he went public with an attack on unnamed individuals showed the depth of his despair. We were in grave danger of losing the team ethic we had developed from the start of the 1990s and our slump in the championship had become alarming, with just five victories in two seasons.

We'd started off well enough in 1995, defeating Somerset at Taunton (where I led the side in Hugh's absence) and then against Northamptonshire in Cardiff, where we chased 287 to get off to our best start in the championship for ten years. We then had an eight-match sequence where we alternated between a draw and a defeat, before losing heavily to Warwickshire, Derbyshire and Essex in quick succession.

My only other match as captain had come against Young Australia at

Neath, where rain wrecked what had looked like a likely victory for us. The Aussies were still more than 200 runs shy of their target with only five wickets left, though a certain Matt Elliott, who was to become our overseas player five years later, was unbeaten on 95. We had lost our way and had no real game-plan. We were the victims of an unusual double that summer when, in successive matches for different teams, the brothers Adrian and Robert Rollins recorded their maiden centuries: Adrian in Derbyshire's 195-run victory over us; and Robert when Essex defeated us by 147 runs at St Helen's.

We were more effective in the one-day game. We finished sixth in the Sunday League after leading the table at the end of June, but we only won one of our last nine matches and fell away. We should have qualified for the quarter-finals of the Benson & Hedges Cup, unable to chase a target of 177 set by Gloucestershire, but the NatWest Trophy again offered us the chance of redemption. Victories over Dorset, Leicestershire and Middlesex – where a quickfire 20 and a brilliant catch by Metto earned him the man-of-the-match award – took us into the semi-final against Warwickshire, who had established themselves as one of the best one-day teams in the country for several years.

Because we were firm underdogs, Hugh decided to break with our normal ritual and book us into a hotel the night before the match so we could work on our game-plan. We found ourselves in the plush surroundings of a large hotel in the middle of Cardiff, but the plan backfired. The players felt more pressurised than relaxed and there was a tension in the air the following morning: I did not get much sleep because my head was spinning from all the information we had digested, Hugh going as far as producing flip charts. We certainly flipped the following day.

It was a repeat of Headingley 1987. In front of a live television audience, we were dismissed for a mere 86. Hugh was the first out for a duck after winning the toss and batting, caught behind off Tim Munton, but television replays showed he had been unfortunate. The rest of us had no excuses. The previous night, we had spoken about the need not to take risky singles to Trevor Penney, a predator in the field who had perfected a technique of picking up the ball quickly and throwing down the stumps, no matter how narrow the angle. David Hemp and I had set about repairing the early damage, moving from 12 for 2 to 34 for 2, when Hemp hit the ball to point and called me for a quick single.

When he saw Penney swooping for the ball, he had a change of heart and sent me back. As I walked back to the pavilion, I could hear spectators having a go at me because, when Penney picked up the ball, I did not make a desperate attempt to get back into my ground. There had been no point: I was not going to beat a direct hit, and if he missed I would have easily made my ground because no one was standing behind the stumps. My only option was to run at a diagonal, onto the square, and hope that his throw hit me, but that would have been a blatant obstruction of the field.

Hemp imploded after that mix-up and ran himself out, with Penney again the marksman. Hemp was to join Warwickshire two seasons later, believing that I had it in for him and that he was not going to get a fair crack under my captaincy. He was a talented left-handed batsman whom I thought should have stayed at Glamorgan and fought for his place. He was his own worst enemy, not me, as he too often put pressure on himself and opponents exploited that all too readily.

In 1996 we had a pre-season tour to South Africa. When we were in Pretoria, Hemp threw a wobbly, slamming his gear down in the changing-room and swearing after being given out. I pulled him to one side and told him that was not the sort of reaction I wanted to see in the dressing-room because it could affect other players. Soon after the start of the campaign, he suffered a serious injury after colliding with Hugh Morris in the outfield during a Benson & Hedges Cup match. He was out for more than a month and when he recovered his fitness, I made him play for the reserves after telling him that no one was just going to walk back into the side.

When he left for Warwickshire I received a lot of criticism from inside and outside the club for not doing more to keep him, but there was little I could do. Hemp had not forgotten his dressing-down in Pretoria and said he was going because he didn't think I was backing him. But his career has not really progressed at Warwickshire. He would have been better off staying and proving his worth with Glamorgan, because he had considerable talent. My attitude was that if any man felt that he had a pre-ordained right to be in the side, he was wise to look elsewhere.

Hemp top scored against Warwickshire with 28 and they took a mere 24.1 overs to knock off the runs for the loss of just two wickets. All over at 3.30 p.m., it was a huge let-down for the crowd. It wasn't so much the fact we had lost, but the manner of our capitulation which was abject. It was little consolation that Warwickshire had made it to their third successive one-day final: we were good enough to have given them a game, but we had now lost three successive one-day semi-finals and were gaining a reputation for being bottlers. We were to make it four before making it to Lord's.

There was little that could be said after Warwickshire. Our only target for the rest of the season was to avoid finishing bottom of the championship, and there was a danger that we were returning to the dark days of the early 1980s – 1993 seemed like a mirage. It was hard to figure out what had gone wrong. That April we had gone on a pre-season tour to Zimbabwe, which had helped us achieve an early momentum when we returned home, winning seven of our first eight matches in all competitions.

There is nothing like a tour for team bonding. We stayed in the same hotel in Harare as fellow tourists Northamptonshire and were due to check out at the same time. The last night had seen a game of Cowboys and Indians, with players from both sides shooting at each other and diving over furniture (some of which did not survive in one piece). Northamptonshire had the good sense to check out early, leaving our tour manager, Mike Fatkin, to pick up the tab for the damages on his credit card at the insistence of the manager of the Monomatapa Hotel.

We boarded a bus for a town called Kwekwe. The words 'EXECUTIVE BUS' adorned the front of the rusting machine: minibus described it and it was the tightest of squeezes on the three-hour journey. When we arrived there, a party was held in our honour and one of the players had discovered that it was the 30th birthday of our physiotherapist, Dean Conway, who is now with the England squad. Deano had kept it quiet and he got a huge shock when he discovered that the locals had made him the guest of honour at the hog roast – an honour which meant that he had to dress up in drag.

Dean is not the slightest of men, as the fact he used to play prop for Cardiff and Mountain Ash would suggest. That gave the men of Kwekwe a problem, until one of them remembered that the wife of the chief was rather a large lady. She happily gave up some of her colourful clothes to Dean, who managed to force his way into them. At least he had the consolation of the roast to look forward to: as guest of honour, he had the first cut. Unfortunately for Deano, the first cut was not the deepest and it only succeeded in chopping off a part of the pig's anatomy I suspect he would not have eaten by choice. He made a gallant effort, chewing through gritted teeth while the rest of us fell about with mirth.

The camaraderie of that tour was replaced by a weary resignation by the end of the summer. I wanted to succeed Hugh as captain, but because the position was in the gift of the committee, there was no way that I could put my name forward. I had to wait to be asked, and I knew that there would be opposition to my appointment by some on the committee because they appreciated that I would be less likely to listen to them than Hugh had been: I had the reputation of being impetuous and a shade rebellious, but at the same time everyone connected with the club needed to be aware that something had to be done.

Some of the counties were beginning to talk in terms of two divisions and we needed to start showing more ambition. To this day, I have no idea whether someone enthusiastically put forward my name or whether it was the case that they could not agree on anyone else: some would probably have preferred Colin Metson, but there was no way that appointment would have been tolerated in the dressing-room and that was one message which did filter its way into the dark recesses of the committee labyrinth.

I set myself the target of finishing in the top five of the championship within two years. It meant changing attitudes and it also demanded that we sign a top name as our overseas player because we had never replaced Viv Richards in kind. Ottis Gibson struggled with injury in 1996 and his dislike of the Cardiff wickets: he was a cricketer who never fulfilled his potential, probably because he didn't appreciate just how much talent he had. As a fast bowler, you need some devil in your heart and that was something Ottis generally lacked.

We did improve in 1996, finishing tenth in the championship, though we declined in one-day cricket. We did make the quarter-finals of the Benson & Hedges Cup which provided us with a return match against Warwickshire at Sophia Gardens. But we blew it again, though not as spectacularly. They set us a target of 240 and we were cruising, Ottis and I both scoring half-centuries. However Warwickshire were a resourceful side then, never beaten until the very end, and they had a poise at the moment of reckoning which we lacked. I was annoyed after being given out leg before by Trevor Jesty for 75, a terrible decision after I had walked down the wicket to Gladstone Small.

Ottis and I had added 136 for the sixth wicket to leave us needing 29 from the last six overs. Even when Ottis was caught on the cover boundary and Darren Thomas was dismissed first ball, I still felt we were in the driving seat. Until Jesty intervened. When he had raised his finger I said to him, 'You must be joking,' before stalking off. At the end-of-match press conference I tore into Jesty, saying that he had made an incompetent decision at the decisive stage of the match. Given that the lbw law states that any benefit of the doubt has to be given to the batsman, how could he say with 100-per-cent certainty that the ball was going to hit the wicket when I was so far out of my crease? The club were not amused and I was hauled before a disciplinary committee – quite rightly, because I had set a bad example – and fined £2,000, suspended for a year pending good behaviour.

The captaincy did not have an adverse affect on my form. I finished with 1,470 runs at 58.80, second only to Tony Cottey in the averages, with five centuries and six fifties. One glance at the averages showed where we were going wrong. We were scoring enough runs, with Hugh Morris and Steve James both making big contributions, but our bowling revolved around Steve Watkin and Robert Croft. They were our attack, Ottis being unable to make any sort of an impact at Sophia Gardens, but my greatest concern was Darren Thomas whose 16 wickets cost 57.75 runs each. His performance was why I decided that Steve Barwick had to be released from the first-team squad: as a bowler, Baz could have gone on for a good few more years, but Darren was the club's future and the lad was throwing it away. It was do or die for him the following season and he needed to understand that.

Also clear was the fact that we required a strike bowler, which was where Waqar Younis came in. The call from his agent was timely because we had identified the need for a paceman. Watty was now in his 30s and if we carried on flogging him as we had been, he would not have lasted much longer. Because Waqar was no all-rounder, though, his presence meant that we had a longer tail – another reason for preferring Adrian Shaw to Metto.

I gave some matches to Adrian in 1996, though Metto was still the undisputed number-one wicket-keeper, but by the time 1997 started I had decided that Adrian was going to be in for the duration. The balance of the side demanded it and so did the atmosphere in the dressing-room. Ironically, we spent the season dressed in Metto's Benefit tie, but sentiment was not going to get in the way of ambition.

The one reservation I had had about taking the captaincy was that it was my Benefit year, but I knew that the chance would probably not come again. I was fortunate to have Paul Russell as my Benefit chairman. He assembled a strong committee and said to me at the start of the year that it would help my cause enormously if I forced my way back into the England squad.

I did the next best thing and played in the six one-day internationals against India and Pakistan. Paul arranged only 26 functions in my Benefit year, which meant that I was not over-extended, and, by aiming for quality rather than quantity, he ensured that those who backed the events had full value for their money. I ended up making more than £150,000.

Despite Paul's urging, I did not expect to be summoned by England. I'd turned 30 and had already been given two chances. David Lloyd had taken over as coach and he was stressing the need for greater continuity. 'Bumble' was big on motivation and beating the patriotic drum. He made for a more positive dressing-room than Keith Fletcher and he showed his emotion, which meant he sometimes put his foot in it when interviewed by the media immediately after a defeat.

We defeated India 3–0 and Pakistan 2–1. I was run out twice against India, suckered by Sachin Tendulkar at Headingley when batting with Graham Thorpe. He hit two to deep square leg and I came for the second in response to his call; except it had not been his call but Tendulkar's. I had naïvely responded to a voice rather than look up to check and it was a dismissal which seemed to sum up my England career.

The international one-dayers were a diversion. At the end of 1996, with Waqar signed and sealed and Duncan Fletcher agreeing to become our coach, I felt it was the year for Glamorgan to make a concerted push for the championship. All the pieces were in place.

14. TAUNTON DECIDER

One of the reasons put forward for my lack of success with England is that I bottle it on the big occasion. Having played a number of significant innings at crucial times for Glamorgan, including a century in the match against Somerset at Taunton in 1997 which we needed to win to clinch the championship title, I would dispute that. International cricket is totally different from the county game: the crowds are bigger, the tension is higher along with the standard and it takes time to adjust.

I was not given that time, like many others and unlike some. Eddie Hemmings once told me that it took him a whole series of six matches before he felt he had come to terms with the demands of Test cricket. My four caps came against the two teams who at the time were the best in the world – West Indies and Australia – and in the case of my first three, the series had already been lost. The bigger the occasion for Glamorgan, the better I respond, as I showed by scoring a century in the 2000 Benson & Hedges Cup final.

Bottler I am not. I am impetuous and I will always look to dominate bowlers, but I have always felt that I had the ability to succeed at the top level. Had David Lloyd or Duncan Fletcher been the England coach when I started my international career in 1988, perhaps it would have turned out differently. That it did not is not something I lose sleep over, because my career is one of fulfilment. Small margins again: as someone who believes in fate, my international career was not meant to be and I am not going to waste my time pretending otherwise. However it did make me chuckle when, after we had won the championship, my name was mentioned as a potential England captain. Was I seen as a Mike Brearley, someone who had to be found a place in the side because of his leadership qualities?

Whereas Hugh Morris had been thorough in his preparations, drawing up a strategy for matches which he followed to the letter, I was far more impulsive. Our first match in 1997 was against Warwickshire in Cardiff and, after they had decided to bat, we rolled them over for 151. A key moment was when I brought on Robert Croft early to have a go at David Hemp, who was making his début for his new county against familiar faces. Crofty is a chirper and I knew he would inflict pressure on Hemp, a batsman more comfortable against seam than spin anyway. The tactic worked – Hemp gave Crofty a return catch first ball.

Steve James and Hugh Morris gave us the perfect start and I eventually declared on 551 for 3. It meant that Warwickshire had failed to claim a bonus point since the system was introduced in 1968. Hugh top scored with an unbeaten 233, an innings which ended when Allan Donald, showing why he was one of the world's finest bowlers, hit him on the helmet with a bouncer of such force that Hugh had to go to hospital for X-rays. It was typical of Donald not to recognise a lost cause: he had just been creamed for four through the covers and, no matter what the score was, he wasn't going to allow anyone to take liberties with him. The bouncer surprised Hugh, depriving him of the split second he needed to react to it, and he ducked into the ball.

Warwickshire were saved by the rain, but we had made our point and Waqar Younis still had to arrive in the country. He was in the dressing-room for our second match, against Yorkshire at Headingley, when rain again deprived us of victory after a Steve James century and incisive bowling by Crofty had put us in a strong position. At the start of the season, I had identified our first three matches as the key to our season because they were against three counties we had traditionally struggled against; and our next match took me back to my old stamping ground in Canterbury.

Duncan Fletcher had spent a lot of time making tail-enders bat in the nets. It was not something we had thought much about. Our last few batsmen in the order had traditionally used their bats to lean on, hoping they would not be required, but Fletch had other ideas, pointing out that in the course of a season there would be three or four matches when they would need to make a contribution if we were to turn draws into victories or defeats into draws.

Canterbury was to prove Fletch right. We slumped to 108 for 6 after I had won the toss and batted, Martin McCague wreaking havoc among our top order. In previous years, we would have struggled to make it to 150, but Crofty, Waqar, Darren Thomas and Steve Watkin all chipped in to take us to 279 – good enough to give us a first innings lead of 125 after Darren and Crofty had done the damage with the ball.

We were well set, especially after 'Sid' James and Adrian Shaw, opening because Hugh had injured his knee, put on 100 for the first wicket. But we slumped to 193 all out and Kent needed 319 to win. They finished the third day on 156 for 3 with Alan Wells still at the wicket. It promised to be a nervous final day. That night, I had a chat with Dean Cosker. I wanted him to bowl over the wicket to Wells rather than round, not aiming at the footmarks outside leg stump, but bowling the ball across the batsman. It worked at the start of the morning and Wells was caught at slip. We bowled them out before lunch to win by 87 runs, with the spinners taking seven wickets between them. Our show was on the road.

I had yet to do anything with the bat and only made 34 after contriving a finish with Hampshire at Cardiff after rain had washed out most of the first day and all of the third. We were set 310 to win and were well placed at 279 for 5 with Gary Butcher and Adrian Shaw salvaging an earlier collapse. The Hampshire captain, John Stephenson (who was to be at the centre of controversy against us in the NatWest Trophy later in the season), started bowling a barrage of bouncers to stop us winning, a tactic he persisted with even after removing Butch. He seemed content with the draw, but he missed out on the chance of victory as we ended up 23 short with only two wickets in hand.

We moved to the top of the table for the first time that season with an innings victory over Durham on another belter of a track at Sophia Gardens. Sid, Hugh and I all scored centuries as we reached 597 for 6 before I declared: it was our highest score in first-class cricket, beating the 587 Glamorgan had scored against Derbyshire in 1951. We had 11 sessions to bowl them out twice and did so with two to spare, Waqar and Watty taking 14 wickets between them. It was a superb effort on a track which favoured the batsmen.

And then Middlesex came to Sophia Gardens, like a ghost in the night. They took a first innings lead of 38 thanks to 96 from Jacques Kallis, who was to be our overseas player two years later, and it had the makings of a close match. And then, in 16 crazy overs from Angus Fraser and James Hewitt, we were dismissed for 31 with only Tony Cottey reaching double figures. It was an extraordinary collapse, the like of which I had never seen before. Fletch and I were laughing on the balcony as wicket followed wicket, most of us finding unusual ways to get out. There were a couple of dubious umpiring decisions, but there was no point in reading the Riot Act in the dressing-room afterwards because it had been just one of those days.

The media reaction surprised me because we were being written off as potential champions. The inquests were long and vituperative. I could not understand the vehemence of the criticism, since it had been our only bad day of the season: a spectacularly bad one, admittedly, but if you are only as good as your last game, it meant we had to bounce back with a victory against Lancashire in Liverpool and the reverse had in no way dented my confidence in the side.

Liverpool was very nearly a wash-out and Sid set a record for being stuck on 99 not out. We were 173 for 1 when rain brought an early end to the first day with Sid one short of the three-figure landmark. He stayed on 99 throughout the second and the third days and for the first session on the final day. The chances of any play looked remote and our travelling supporters gave up on the idea of seeing any cricket, having arrived late on the first day, and went off on a tour of the *Coronation Street* set.

Play eventually got under way after lunch and I agreed a target of 273 with the Lancashire captain Neil Fairbrother, who organised some declaration bowling which Sid tucked into to finish unbeaten on 152. We had 60 overs to bowl them out and that meant Waqar firing. He had done well in his six weeks for us, but he had yet to take a game by the scruff of its neck and we needed him to fire. The result was a career-best 7 for 25 for him and he became the first Glamorgan bowler since his fellow Pakistani Majid Khan in 1969 to take a hat-trick for the county.

He took two wickets in his first over and we never looked back. There are few finer sights in cricket than Waqar running in from his mark, which is closer to the boundary than it is to the wickets. One of the reasons I had been so keen to sign him is that he bowled a fuller length than most fast bowlers, the master of reverse swing, and I felt he would not be disheartened by the slow wickets in Cardiff. He was the perfect foil for Watty and the pair took 129 wickets between them with a virtually identical average.

Liverpool was not the turning point of our 1997 season: it was the defining moment because after it all the players knew we were genuine title contenders. It was also the scene of one of our many Darren Thomas stories.

Darren had matured under the influence of Fletch and was at last turning potential into performance. One of the reasons I had been so keen to wean him from Steve Barwick's influence was that, as a player, he is a captain's dream. He would do anything for you, but he had to learn to look after himself and not be content with being a player on the fringes, getting a game every now and then. He was far better than that, but I am not sure that he recognised that. He is also an uplifting presence in the dressing-room and the butt of many jokes. *Private Eye* have Colemanballs; at Glamorgan we have Thomasballs because he continually comes out with the outrageous. For instance, when we were at Kwekwe in 1995, Darren was tucking into the hog roast with relish and decided that he fancied another plateful. 'Hey, Butch,' he called over to Gary Butcher. 'Cut me another slice of beef off that pig.' Cue laughter.

Now, when we go away we eat out as a team on a given night: in Liverpool it was Darren's turn to book the restaurant. He reported back to me that he had found the perfect place, French and posh in his words. So we all got into our best clobber, apart from the recipient of the Dick of the Day award – which is handed out before we go out for a meal to the most worthy recipient for an act of gross stupidity – who had to wear a loud and tasteless shirt. The players were keen to know where we were going.

'Posh nosh,' said Darren. 'It's a French place called Merci Vous. New cuisine and all that stuff.'

He had obtained directions and off we set in a convoy of taxis. When we arrived we thought we had found the wrong place. The waterside that Darren had talked about looked more like a swamp and, far from nouvelle cuisine, it was apparent that we were going to be treated to Beefeater's best. He had booked us into a place called the Mersey View.

There is something about Darren and water. When he and Wayne Law were travelling to The Oval by car, they were near the hotel when they crossed a bridge over a large stretch of water. 'What river is that?' asked Wayne. Darren shrugged his shoulders: 'Not got a clue.' They were so anxious to find out the name of the river that they asked some of the boys in the hotel. More laughter – the secret of dressing-room harmony and definitely the best medicine.

Darren came good in our following match against Sussex at St Helen's. We had been put in to bat and were bowled out for 172 after rain had washed out the first two sessions, Crofty and Adrian Shaw scoring valuable runs in the middle order. We were looking down the barrel against a side that was near the bottom of the table, only for Waqar to go one better than he'd done in Liverpool. He took 8 for 17, another career-best, and was unplayable with his quick, late-swinging deliveries. We had so often been on the wrong end of an overseas fast bowler that it was a joy to reflect from the slips on what Waqar had brought to the side. Sussex's 54 gave us a healthy first-innings lead. We were 148 for 2 in our second innings, Sid and I adding 119 for the third wicket, when I ran myself out and we crashed to 183 for 9 before I declared. Sussex had to score 302 to win and I could not see them getting anywhere near that.

They saw off Waqar, but Darren claimed 5 for 24, a career-best with Crofty and Watty picking up the other wickets as Sussex were skittled for 67: we had taken their 20 wickets in less than 56 overs and were back in the top three of the table. Our next match was also at St Helen's. While Sussex had been struggling, Gloucestershire were one of our rivals for the title. Like us, they had surprised the pundits and it was a match we could not afford to lose. Hugh hit 173 to take us to maximum batting points and a polished display in the field forced Gloucestershire to follow on. Dean Cosker took four wickets in their second innings to leave us just 48 to win in 21 overs, Sid hitting the winning runs – and a spectator – with a six. We led the table by 17 points.

We were then outplayed by Derbyshire at Chesterfield after I had blundered by putting them in on a greenish wicket which I thought would do a bit early on: 247 for no wicket told a different story and we would have had to follow on but for a typically battling century by Tony Cottey. We also wobbled against Nottinghamshire at Colwyn Bay. We reduced them to 159 for 8 on the final day, which gave them a lead of eight; but we failed to take a wicket in the final session and had to settle for a draw, which made victory in our next match against Worcestershire essential if we were not to lose ground.

We ended up chasing 374 to win in a minimum of 81 overs after centuries by Tim Curtis in their first innings and Philip Weston in the second (after he had been dropped early on) put the home side in command. We were 155 for 6 in our first innings, 321 behind Worcestershire, when I played one of my finest innings for Glamorgan. Everything went right for me and I finished unbeaten on 161. The former England batsman Tom Graveney said it was the best knock he had ever seen at the ground, a big compliment given the era he played in and the many Graeme Hick centuries he had witnessed.

It was not enough, however. Weston's reprieve meant we were always up against it. I could have pulled up and played for the draw, but I felt we had to go for the 16 points. We scored our runs at a much faster rate than Worcestershire, but ended up 55 short despite a century by Steve James. I took some criticism for the defeat, but I was by then not interested in a top-three finish. We went back to the top of the table after beating Northamptonshire at Abergavenny. I dislocated my finger in the field and, with Tony Cottey having been dropped, Waqar Younis led the side for the second half of the match. I thought he would take the chance to rest himself in the field, given the slow wicket. However he bowled us to victory, taking ten wickets in the match, while Sid continued his good form with a century in each innings. We were back on top.

There were four games to go, the first against the reigning champions, Leicestershire. They turned out to be the raining champions in 1997 because no county lost more play to the weather than the Foxes. The final day at Grace Road was sunny, but because the covers had leaked there was no chance of any play and we had to settle for a draw. It was the same outcome at The Oval against Surrey, a match we should have won after taking a first-innings lead of 234. We reduced Surrey to 95 for 4 in their second innings, but Graham Thorpe played superbly for 222 and we ended up needing 254 to win in around 40 overs. We had an early look at it but, with Surrey still in the race for the title, I was not going to hand them 16 points on a plate and we put the shutters up.

The Surrey captain, Adam Hollioake, complained afterwards that we had cheated the crowd by not going for victory, but he could hardly talk. He had chosen to bat on, rather than declare, and with two international spinners in the Surrey side – Saqlain Mushtaq and Ian Salisbury – there was only going to be one winner in a chase on a turning wicket. Surrey's coach, Dave Gilbert, also weighed in with some insulting remarks, but I had no reason to apologise to anybody. Surrey are a club who put themselves first, second and third and I let their moaning wash over me. They were out of the championship race, but with Kent defeating Gloucestershire, we were 12 points behind in second place with two to play.

One concern was the weather. We had two matches to play, against Essex in Cardiff and Somerset in Taunton, while Kent were finishing off in Canterbury and the South East was traditionally drier than the west. We dominated the first two days against Essex, making 361 and forcing them to follow on. They did better the second time around and an unbeaten 98 from Paul Grayson took them to 340. We were left with 149 to win on a deteriorating wicket.

Smaller targets are often harder to reach than larger ones. It's all in the mind and you tend to think small, batting with caution instead of getting on with it. Before we knew it, we were 26 for 3 and I had been dropped before scoring. Tony Cottey joined me at the wicket and we somehow managed to survive until lunch, playing and missing and looking unsure of ourselves. Fletch had a word with us during the break and told us to play normally and not worry about the circumstances.

It worked and within an hour we had won by seven wickets. I was delighted for Cotts, because he had not had one of his best seasons with the bat and was feeling guilty that he hadn't contributed to the championship effort. He had done, of course, but it took that vital unbeaten 35 to convince him. We were back on top of the table with all to play for at Taunton and I was delighted to present Darren Thomas with his county cap after he had started the year playing for his job.

And so to Taunton. We bowled them out for 252 on the first day, with Waqar taking four wickets and Watty three. The weather was gloomy and, after we had lost two quick wickets, I told Hugh to drop anchor while I got on with it. We finished the day on 159 for 2, but play the following day was held up until after lunch because of rain. The umpires refused to give up hope of play and when we got back on in the gloom, I hit my first ball from Andy Caddick for four and went on to reach my century without hitting a single. It was all or nothing by that stage because Kent were well on top in their final match.

We closed the day on 353 for 4. I had made 142 and Hugh was unbeaten on 136. The third day, a Saturday, was much brighter and with Crofty hitting 86 and Hugh eventually out for 165, we were dismissed for 527 – a lead of 275. I told the bowlers to let rip, but Waqar was struggling with a virus and his 11 overs were smashed for 84 runs. Somerset made a rapid start, 60 being put on for the first wicket in no time. Enter Darren Thomas, who took five quick wickets to leave Somerset reeling at 166 for 7. The championship was surely ours.

Graham Rose and Andy Caddick had other ideas and put on 95 for the eighth wicket as play looked certain to go into the final day when we would be at the mercy of the weather. Watty got rid of Rose to a catch behind, which the batsman disputed, and he and Dean Cosker quickly took the last two wickets to leave us needing 11 to win and claim our first championship title since 1969.

Caddick wasn't going to give us anything and had a couple of loud appeals before Sid hit the winning runs and Taunton resounded to the chanting of Welsh supporters. The champagne flowed and it was without any doubt the high point of my career. Duncan Fletcher, a Zimbabwean who supported the Springboks, wore a Welsh rugby jersey that we had presented him with and the party went on all night. We had beaten Kent by four points. When I was asked afterwards if we would have won the title without Fletch, I said it was an impossible question to answer – other than to say he was worth many more than four points to us.

15. FLETCH - MARK TWO

Of all the appointments made by Glamorgan during my time with the club, the best was Duncan Fletcher. When you consider the likes of Viv Richards, Waqar Younis, Jacques Kallis, Matthew Elliott and Alan Butcher, that is saying something. I have to confess that at the first mention of him in 1996, when we were looking for a coach, it did not ring any bells with me. The surname Fletcher only conjured up images I would have preferred to stay locked in the deepest recesses of my memory bank.

Steve James first mentioned Fletch's name after spending a couple of winters playing in Zimbabwe. Fletch was coaching Western Province in Cape Town and had made his name as a player when he captained Zimbabwe in the inaugural World Cup in 1983, scoring an unbeaten 69 and taking 6 for 42 in the shock victory over Australia at Trent Bridge. A left-handed batsman and right-arm medium-quick bowler, he was rated as one of the finest fielders in the history of the game.

In the summer of 1996 he coached the South Africa A side on their tour of Britain. They played Glamorgan in Cardiff and won by an innings and 44 runs inside two days. We made contact with him and he expressed an interest in coming over. Warwickshire were also interested in securing his signature because Bob Woolmer was leaving Edgbaston to take over as coach of South Africa. I suspect that he recommended Fletch as his successor at Warwickshire, but we'd got in first and Fletch remained loyal to us.

I hit it off with him immediately even though – or possibly because – we were totally different characters. I was outgoing and headstrong, while Fletch was quiet and reflective. When it came to cricket we were on the same wavelength and he had firm ideas about the way the partnership between a coach and his captain should work. He thought the coach should act as consultant to the captain and provide a shoulder to lean on. The captain had to be given the responsibility for selecting the side, because he was the one who had to make the decisions on the field, and never once did Fletch take issue with one of my decisions. He would always back me to the hilt even if he reckoned he would have taken a different course in my position.

John Derrick had been the first-team coach in 1996. When the plaudits were heaped on Fletch, and rightly so, after our 1997 championship success, I felt for John. He has an astute cricketing brain and I am sure that his time as the Glamorgan coach will come. He had done an excellent job with the reserves and youngsters, but I felt that he was not always strict enough with the senior squad because he had played in the same side as a number of us. When the survivors of the campaigns in the 1980s and the early 1990s (like myself) have gone, John will have his opportunity.

Fletch thought differently to anyone I had ever met in cricket. He was feverishly enthusiastic about the game and he used to come to my house and talk long into the night about ways of getting around the rules, often coming up with ingenious and outrageous ideas. He changed our training methods and placed a greater emphasis on fitness. He encouraged us to play soccer or rugby before and after a match – this irritated some supporters who said we should be concentrating on cricket, and the letters poured in. Fletch was not put off. His reasoning was that as well as helping foster team spirit, the matches also brought out the competitive instinct of players which he felt was essential to success. He would cleverly divide up the teams: young against old was his favourite and the tackles would fly in. Fletch would act as referee and you could see that he loved it. We picked up a few injuries, but nothing serious.

The fiercest matches were the ones after the first and second days of our championship decider against Somerset at Taunton. They were full-blooded affairs, with players getting rid of their pent-up aggression, and they showed just how much more competitive as a unit we had become under Fletch – a quality which helped us turn around several difficult situations: we bailed each other out and while supporters may have thought we were wasting time having a kick-about, Fletch had appreciated their therapeutic and psychological value. Again, it is something that other counties have since taken on board.

When I took over as captain I used to ask the players to stay up to 30 minutes in the dressing-room afterwards so we could mull over the day's play: if anyone wanted to get anything off his chest, that was the time to do it. When I started playing, everyone would go straight into the bar after getting changed, chatting to the opposition and the umpires. However, as the game has become more professional, players have tended to drift off at the end of a day and an integral part of the game's tapestry has been unravelled.

I remember beer being served at lunch at Headingley, uncapped bottles lined up in a row, but it is all energy drinks and water nowadays. I caused a stir in 1998 in the final session of a boring draw on a dead wicket at Durham when I asked the twelfth man to bring on halves of lager for anyone who had a thirst which needed quenching. Interaction between sides is something I would dearly like to see rekindled, though the chances are remote, but I felt that we were losing something as a team by allowing players to change and disappear at the end of a day's play when we were at home. The talks brought us closer together, but Fletch's soccer games were even better. As usual, he had got it spot on.

When we played Northamptonshire at Abergavenny in 1997, Fletch put on his socks after taking a shower, only to find that they came up to his knees. Robert Croft had cut the toes off both socks and everyone in the dressing-room fell about. Fletch was not amused and had a face like thunder. The room suddenly went quiet and, when he discovered who the culprit was, he pulled Crofty to one side and gave him a dressing down.

I was surprised at Fletch's reaction and told him so later. He felt that his authority had been undermined, that he had been made to look a fool in front of those to whom he was meant to be an example. I told him that nothing could have been further from the truth – the prank was a mark of respect which showed that he had been accepted by the players – but it was a rare occasion when I struggled to get through to him.

He was still a bit off when we went up to Leicestershire for our next match. Steve Watkin's 7 for 41 had put us in a strong position, but poor drainage and leaky covers put an early end to the match. We all went out for a meal and our physiotherapist, Dean Conway, had won the Dick of the Day award: he had to wear a garish skin-tight top which Tony Cottey, a good foot shorter than Dean, would have struggled to coax round his shoulders. Dean looked absurd and the rest of the diners all had a good laugh at his expense. Crofty got up to do his party piece, 'Alouette', and stood on a chair. He immediately fell through it and the place erupted. Fletch laughed the loudest, the affair of the socks finally forgotten.

Fletch was not one for letting his hair down in front of the players. I often used to go out for a meal with him and the club secretary Mike Fatkin, but there were two occasions when Fletch did let himself go in the players' company. The first was in Liverpool in 1997 when rain had brought play to an early end on the first day and, as it was hammering down outside, it was obvious we were not going to start the following morning. Everyone gave it a lash.

I had gone out for a meal with Fletch, Mike Fatkin and Adrian Dale. When we returned, the players were still in the bar and Duncan joined in the drinking. After a while he turned to Gordon Lewis, who was standing in as scorer for Byron Denning, and said, 'Hey, Gordon, are you on the Glamorgan committee?' Gordon, the most mild-mannered of men, muttered a yes in response and you knew he was trying to work out what Fletch's follow-up would be.

'Well, you're a f***ing spy so f*** off,' hinted Fletch, not the most fervent of believers in the committee system. All the players burst out laughing, wondering if their ears had been deceiving them. Gordon stammered and mopped his brow, saying that there was no way he would be reporting back to the committee that the players were up drinking past midnight: he had not seen anything. As he was speaking, the lift door kept opening and shutting with a very drunk Hugh Morris unable to focus clearly enough to punch the button to his floor. Hugh very rarely got into a state like that and the twelfth man, Alun Evans, had a go at him, forgetting that even if there had been any play the next day, Hugh would have been putting his feet up having already been dismissed. We had been rolled out for 31 by Middlesex the previous match and Fletch saw the value in allowing the players to let themselves go a bit. That morning Fletch and I went to the ground, leaving the players having a lie-in, to confirm what we already knew: no play today.

The only other occasion I saw Fletch the worse for wear was during his second season with us in 1999. It was during the World Cup and a lunch was held in Cardiff in honour of the Australian team. Fletch was sitting next to Steve James and neither man was renowned for his drinking exploits. For some reason, they decided to get into a speed-red-wine-drinking contest and bottles of the stuff were disappearing as fast as the waiters could uncork them. I was pleased to see the pair of them relaxing and the enjoyment carried on afterwards at a pub in Cardiff. Sid soon made his excuses and staggered into a taxi: he later said that when he got home he wandered up his neighbour's drive by mistake. Fletch stayed and put away a few pints of lager.

He managed to stay in control, just about, until he decided that he felt peckish. The only nourishment to hand was growing in window boxes and Fletch was soon munching away on petunias, bringing the house down in the process. For someone as deeply absorbed in the game as he was, and is, he appreciated that there are times when players need to unwind. It was a question of timing.

He was the best man-manager I have ever worked with. He quickly identified players as individuals and treated them differently. He was harder on some than he was on others – recognising those who needed a kick up the backside when they were on the ground and those who needed a helping hand. We only used 14 players that summer. It was a happy side to be a part of and no one was in a hurry to give up his place.

Fletch salvaged the career of Darren Thomas, spending hours in the nets and offering advice at every opportunity. Darren has since been on two England A tours and he's a good example of how Fletch could refine raw material. Some in the club had given hope of ever making something of Darren, feeling he was a lost cause. Fletch came to a contrary view after just a few minutes of watching him. Telling Darren that I had left him out of the team to play Gloucestershire in the 2000 Benson & Hedges Cup final was the worst moment of my time as captain.

Selection is not personal and, with Alex Wharf establishing himself in our one-day side after joining from Nottinghamshire, there was no place for Darren in that Cup final. But having to tell him and see his disappointment was worse than facing Courtenay Walsh on a lively wicket. Darren was not one to sulk, though. He would have jumped through a ring of fire for Glamorgan. He bounced back and, typically, clinched our promotion to the championship's first division at the end of the summer.

The way Fletch reacted to our dismissal for 31 by Middlesex played a pivotal part in our success in 1997. He laughed as the wickets tumbled. Any anxiety, disappointment or even anger that he felt was not transmitted to the players. In the team-talk after the game, there were no accusations. He said that it had been one of those days when everything had gone wrong. All teams suffered from them, but only the good ones bounced back. We left the dressing-room feeling positive despite the embarrassing performance and that was the essence of Fletch: he would make a short man feel tall, a fat man think he was slim and an ordinary player feel that he was Don Bradman or Ian Botham.

Fletch often took a player to the pub for a quiet chat to get away from the ground and a cricket environment and he always stressed the need for enjoyment. One of the things I resented as a player was a punishment known as 'naughty-boy nets', which used to be ordered after a poor team performance. Some players had to drive in a long way for the net and their resentment too often showed. No benefit was served, other than to help calm the anger of whoever called them, and Fletch not only agreed with my decision to get rid of them, but cleverly laid the emphasis on the positive. He drew up a timetable for nets and training, which often included a day after a match. The players knew the schedule in advance, so if we suffered a bad defeat or scraped a draw, there was less moaning about having to come into the club the following day because it had not been laid down as time off. But if we had played well, Fletch would tell the boys not to bother coming in the following day: he was more carrot than stick, but not to the point where he was a pushover. He had no time for anyone who was wasting his talent. He was simply a coach who knew when to say what.

We missed Fletch when he decided to take the summer of 1998 off.

He'd not had a break for three years and we slipped to 12th in the championship. We were plagued by injuries, the most serious case being Waqar Younis who played four matches before having to return to Pakistan with an elbow problem. Only Steve James scored runs with any consistency. Our one-day form was no better.

It was the last summer of the one-division Sunday League. We finished tenth, one place away from a place in the new first division. It was a slightly false position. We won our final three matches having never appeared to be in with a shout of forcing our way into the top half of the table. We did not win our first match until the end of May and we left it too late to put together a winning run.

We needed Fletch to return for 1999, but no sooner was he in Wales than he was being linked to the job of England coach which had been vacated by David Lloyd. There was some opposition in the media to the idea of a foreigner being given the job, though it had worked well for the Wales rugby team who had prospered under the New Zealander Graham Henry, and the South African cricket team had hardly suffered for having the Englishman Bob Woolmer as coach. Whispers about who was on the England and Wales Cricket Board's shortlist grew into informed rumours. Fletch confided to me that not only had he been approached but that he had also had an interview. He asked my opinion. It was one of the top jobs in cricket, never mind how low England had fallen, and I felt he would regret it for the rest of his life if he turned it down because he would always ask himself, 'What if?' From my experience with England, I knew that Duncan was exactly the sort of coach England needed.

When he was appointed, there were some who assumed that I would get back into the England squad, perhaps even as captain, but that was not the way Fletch worked. He would never lay himself open to accusations of bias and I knew deep down that my chances of getting back into the five-day reckoning were virtually extinct because of my age. The one-day game was different, and I was very upset when I didn't make the squad for the triangular series between England, West Indies and Zimbabwe in the summer of 2000 after becoming the first player to hit a century in both the semi-final and final of a knock-out tournament.

Fletch told me afterwards that the squad had been chosen long before my century against Gloucestershire at Lord's but was withheld from the media for three weeks. I was eventually called up to replace Nasser Hussain, but I had taken the disappointment to heart and got myself into a bad run of form. My brief time back in the fold showed how Fletch's influence had been profound – the emphasis being on the team rather than individuals – and England have become competitive again.

Unfortunately 1999 was nothing like 1997 for Glamorgan. It was the last year of the old championship, which was being split into two divisions the following year. Needing to finish in the top half of the table to make the new first division, we failed miserably. We finished 14th and for the second season running did not have our overseas player for the full season (Jacques Kallis only played six championship matches for us because of the World Cup and injury).

Some of the Glamorgan players felt that Fletch should have left Glamorgan the moment he had accepted the England job, but there was no way I was having that. He was too good a man to lose at such a crucial time and, anyway, he wanted to stay. It was hard for him, especially with the media wondering what he was doing with Glamorgan when England were floundering against New Zealand. Unlike some, Fletch retained his professionalism and the fact that our season proved a relative failure was down to the players, not him.

Our best victory of the campaign was against Yorkshire at Headingley in September. We defeated them by an innings and it was the first time we had won a first-class match at the ground. I had scored 186, but Fletch was taken with Michael Vaughan who had made a mere single in each innings. 'There is something about him that I like,' said Fletch. Nobody else had had time to see it; but Vaughan has gone on to prove himself as an international cricketer under Fletch.

I was worried that I was on borrowed time as captain and decided to stand down at the end of the season. We had lost some of our competitive edge and I had been rocked by crowd protests after our NatWest Trophy quarter-final defeat against Gloucestershire at Sophia Gardens. I'd made a dreadful mistake after misreading the green wicket: I put them into bat, only to see Tim Hancock and Kim Barnett put on 142 for the first wicket. Gloucestershire posted 274 for 6 in their 55 overs, 46 runs coming off the last 19 balls after we had fought back, and it was a target we never looked like getting. We ended up beaten by 136 runs.

A small section of the crowd reacted by hurling abuse at us, tearing down the Welsh flag we had draped over our balcony and spitting on it. They abused our elderly dressing-room attendant and the players were so shaken that they did not want to leave the dressing-room for the presentation ceremony. I had never experienced anything like it at Glamorgan: we had played badly and the supporters had every right to feel upset, but the antics of a few drunken louts should not have had such an impact. The club identified them and took appropriate action.

The players took the abuse personally, but there was no message of support from the committee and I felt then that it was time to go as captain. Fletch could not offer much in the way of guidance because he was not going to be around and that was another factor in my decision: how could I work with another coach after Fletch? The Glamorgan secretary, Mike Fatkin, as usual offered his support – he was the one guy with the club who would always telephone me or call round after a major disappointment, cracking a joke to get me smiling again and making me feel better about myself. I would not have lasted five years as captain if Mike hadn't been around.

The committee eventually gave me their backing by asking me to carry on, but it was only when I went to Ireland with the players at the end of the season that I started to waver. The boys, to a man, said they wanted me at the helm as we attempted to get into the first division of the championship at the first attempt. I was still not persuaded; but I then talked it over with Sue, who questioned whether deep down I really wanted to quit, and my Mum, who told me bluntly to stop messing about and accept the offer.

Mum knows best, as they say, but it was never going to be the same without Fletch. There were times when I did something on the field, such as put a fielder in a different position or make a surprise bowling change, and expected Fletch to query it afterwards. He would sometimes ask me why I had taken a particular course of action and, occasionally, I would admit that I did not know – something in my head just told me to.

'I love that,' he would say. 'Trust your instincts and never be afraid of being different.' It is to Glamorgan's considerable benefit that we did so after Steve James had brought up the name of Duncan Fletcher.

16. COMMITTED, NOT COMMITTEED

It's a safe bet that when I retire I will not be seeking election to join the Glamorgan committee. The only reason I would have for doing so would be to support any move to change the way the club is organised from an unwieldy group of amateurs to a board of directors where the roles of everyone involved in the club would be clearly defined.

There were times during my period of captaincy when I did not know where I stood and by the end of my five years in charge the job had become a burden. Even if the committee had said at the end of the 2000 season that I would have total autonomy to run the side as I saw fit without being accountable to them, I would still have retired back to the ranks. I had had enough.

Things had changed in my last year anyway. Hugh Davies had stepped down as the chairman of the cricket committee. We'd had one last battle when I argued that the club should sign opening bowler Alex Wharf from Nottinghamshire. Alex had a young family and wanted the security of a three-year contract. Hugh felt that two years was ample for a player who had already played for two counties without winning his cap with either. He had a point, in that Glamorgan had made some misguided signings in the past, but I said I was prepared to stake my reputation on Alex proving himself with Glamorgan.

I had approached him after Glamorgan's match with Nottingham-shire in 1999 in Colwyn Bay. In that game I'd come to the wicket when we were 503 for 3 on our way to our highest-ever score in first-class cricket, 648. We had bowled out Nottinghamshire, who were near the foot of the table, for 228 and were well on our way to an innings victory. We had had them at 9 for 6 on the opening morning before Alex came in and hammered 78 to take his side to a respectable total. A quietly spoken Yorkshireman, he was someone who did not recognise a lost cause. He was bowling when I came to the wicket and at that stage I was expecting the bowlers to be going through the motions after three Glamorgan players had hit centuries. Wharf had other ideas and he gave it everything he had, throwing in a few verbals as well. It struck me then that that sort of competitive edge – the refusal to throw in the towel no matter how hopeless the position seemed – was what we needed and at the end of that day I congratulated him on his performance. When I heard at the end of the season that he was available, I wasted no time in making a move.

Alex was keen to come, but the sticking point was Hugh Davies. Just as he had refused to budge over Tony Cottey, and how we missed his presence in 1999, so he said that Wharf was not worth more than the offer of a two-year contract. I felt that he was merely opposing me: my hunch was based on more than his and I appealed directly to the committee. Alex was offered a three-year deal. He quickly repaid our faith, helping us get to Lord's in the Benson & Hedges Cup final, and he recorded personal bests with both the bat and the ball in first-class cricket.

It was an argument which should not have happened. I was not in the habit of asking the committee to sign players for the sake of it, but we had fallen from the heights of 1997 by not strengthening the squad: Hugh Morris and Cotts had gone and I did not want to see a repeat of the early 1970s when we fell from county champions to whipping-boys alarmingly quickly. The committee needed to show ambition.

Hugh Davies was replaced as the chairman of the cricket committee at the start of the 2000 season by Ricky Needham. When I'd joined Glamorgan in 1984, I was assigned to the St Fagan's club on the outskirts of Cardiff, playing for them in the Western League on any Saturday when I was not required by Glamorgan. Ricky was the club's captain: a powerful left-handed batsman, he had made one appearance for Glamorgan in the 1970s and was deemed good enough to have carved out a career as a professional, though he chose to answer the calling of the law.

Ricky, an Old Harrovian, had a presence about him. Hugh Davies had made 52 appearances for Glamorgan in the 1950s, long before my time. I could not respect him as a player, so I needed to be able to respect him as a person, but that never happened. It was different with Ricky, whose attitude was that he did not seek to interfere in the running of the team. All he wanted was that I gave him my reasons for making decisions, so he could be armed in committee meetings. It made for a healthy relationship.

Despite that, I went into the 2000 season knowing that it would be my last as captain. I was mentally and physically tired and being the captain of a county is about far more than leading the side on the field or picking the team. I wanted to spend more time with my family and spend time developing a career off the field to prepare for my retirement. Leading Glamorgan had been the highlight of my career, but there was nothing to be gained in carrying on for the sake of it. In Steve James, Adrian Dale and Robert Croft, there were three players I felt were all ready to replace me and Sid was offered the job by the committee at the end of the season.

Despite my run-ins with Hugh Davies, my chief objection to the committee was not personal, but the fact they were there at all. Most of them had jobs and I could imagine their reaction if I told them how their businesses should be run: they would have asked what I knew about it. Precisely. I only ever went to one meeting of the club's executive committee. There were some important cricket issues on the agenda and the discussion went on for more than two hours. The cricket matters were glossed over quickly, but the trivia took a lot longer and I struggled to disguise my boredom.

When I took over as captain, I asked the committee to appoint someone full-time to look after the recruitment side. Graham Reynolds had good contacts in schools and attracted players like Dean Cosker and Owen Parkin to the club, but I wanted someone who would get around other counties and see who was coming through their academies and local leagues. No decision was ever made and I think we will pay for it. The Glamorgan committee is struggling to come to terms with the changing nature of first-class cricket. The old boy network is withering and the sport is becoming far more hard-nosed. Clubs like Glamorgan are fighting for their future. It will not be long before there is a transfer system in cricket and it will become more and more important to sign up players when they are young. Tradition is on its way out, along with the saying, 'It is just not cricket'.

The counties which succeed are those which are run properly with a clearly defined chain of command. Having a committee of 24 is not the way forward and as a club we have to start anticipating what the future will look like. There will be pressure to change the system of three up and three down in the championship: the system was adopted because it was the only way that the England and Wales Cricket Board could get enough votes for the change to two divisions, along with the promise that counties would continue to get an equal split from the Test match proceeds.

Neither policy will stand the test of time. There will be calls for only two clubs to go down followed by one. The clubs in English rugby's premier division demanded in 2000 to be ring-fenced for five years to allow them the time to develop as businesses and they all receive far more money from their union than the clubs in the division below them. How long before similar cries are heard in cricket?

I have sat on committees. I was a member of the England and Wales Cricket Board's umpires committee which decided which umpires would get what matches. We had a discussion about the 1998 NatWest Trophy final and the usual policy was to give the match to the two umpires who had scored the highest marks during the season. There was a call for Nigel Plews to stand in the match, even though he was not in the top two.

I suggested that his impending retirement could be marked by appointing him the third umpire. It seemed a logical suggestion. If umpires go into a season knowing that their performances will be rewarded by being given a showpiece final, giving it to Plews, whom I respected as a fair umpire who got things right far more often than not, would render the marking system redundant. I was told that Plews would not make a good third umpire. Why not? – 'He struggles to see the monitor.' I burst into laughter. The fact that if he struggled to watch a television screen would suggest he might have some difficulty working out what might have happened 22 yards in front of him seemed lost on the board.

Just as I couldn't contemplate seeking election to the Glamorgan committee, so I cannot imagine myself ever becoming an umpire. It is becoming an increasingly thankless job, even if it is better paid now than before. At the captains' meeting at the end of the 2000 season, there was a concern that the standards of umpiring in the championship were declining. One captain of a first division team said he could not understand why there were more and more lbw decisions being given when the quality of wickets had deteriorated. Given that any benefit of the doubt had to be given to batsmen, he wondered how umpires could raise their finger so often when the ball was doing all sorts of things.

I think it was more of a problem in the first division than in the second. We played on a few shocking tracks – the one at Bristol in particular could have cost Gloucestershire points because it had clearly not been prepared properly – and of course there were decisions that went against us, but that has been the same every year. Over the course of a season, things usually average themselves out. I thought the point about lbws was well made: as a batsman I would say that, but I think it illustrates how much tougher umpiring has become.

The game is more aggressive today than it was ten years ago, let alone 20 or 30. There have always been fiery individuals – W.G. Grace was hardly an admirer of umpires and in post-war years Glamorgan's Wilf Wooller raised the hackles of opponents with his gamesmanship – but the challenge to authority is now more collective. Wooller was a natural competitor, but defeat did not mean that much to a number of players then, with the game made up of amateurs as well as professionals.

The England and Wales Cricket Board has called on captains to control their players and make sure they assume responsibility when things get heated on the field. I had few problems as Glamorgan captain, though there was one incident which made the lead item on *News at Ten*, cited as evidence of the deteriorating discipline of cricketers. We were playing Essex at Chelmsford in the 1997 NatWest Trophy semi-final and a tight match was nearing its end.

We had made 301 for 9 in our 60 overs, Steve James leading the way with a century. Essex had made a rapid start with Stuart Law and Darren Robinson putting on 150 for the first wicket. There had been an altercation when Darren Thomas accidentally sent down a beamer to

Law, who reacted in typically Australian fashion by letting rip a volley of abuse. Darren had tried to calm him down by saying it was an accident – which it was – but Law lost it and all the toys came out of his pram in an incident which did a fine player little credit.

Play went on beyond 8 p.m., because of two interruptions for rain, and the light was fading. Essex needed six to win off 41 balls with two wickets left. Mark Ilott was batting and he complained to the umpires about the light. Robert Croft, a friend of Ilott's, told him in no uncertain terms to shut up and get on with it. Ilott marched down the wicket waving his bat and exchanged insults with Croft. Things got a bit heated, but it was something and nothing and certainly did not justify making the lead item on *News at Ten*.

That was a big match for both sides. It was our third semi-final of the 1990s and we were determined not to make it a hat-trick of defeats. Essex, coming to terms with life after Graham Gooch, had not had the greatest of seasons in the championship and it was their one chance of winning a trophy that season. With the game so finely balanced, players were bound to be at their most competitive and, as a captain, I was not going to rebuke Crofty for his fierce will to win.

The umpires conferred about the light as Ilott and Croft continued their discussion and they decided to take the players off. It was the right decision, in the sense that the light was fading, but Essex had won the toss and decided to field so there was also a case for making them carry on. We returned the following morning and, after the start was delayed by 30 minutes because of rain, Darren Thomas took a wicket to leave Essex needing three runs with Peter Such – the proverbial number 11 in a team of number 11s – walking to the wicket. I felt we were going to Lord's, but an attempted yorker from Darren allowed Such to hit him for four through extra cover and we had failed in another semi-final.

Ilott and Croft were fined by their counties before the England and Wales Cricket Board decided to intervene: trial by television. The pair were put on probation after the media had gone to town about how cricket was no longer a game for gentlemen, but there had been no need for the board to get involved. It was something that happened in the heat of the moment and you cannot always expect players to act rationally at times of high emotion.

Part of cricket's problem is the way that it is perceived, as a genteel English pastime. The Welsh boxing champion Joe Calzaghe once said that he did not regard cricket as a sport. Well, I wouldn't fancy facing Joe in the boxing ring, but if he were to swap his boxing gloves for a pair of cricket ones and stand at the crease with Courtney Walsh or Glenn McGrath thundering in at him, I think he might be tempted to change his mind. Cricket is not a soft sport: it is physically and mentally demanding and much of it is played in the head.

Because cricket is about small margins, players will try it on. The umpires' job is not enviable, but their decisions have to be respected at the time they are made, which is why Glamorgan were right to discipline me in 1996 when I had a go at Trevor Jesty on the field. The England captain, Nasser Hussain, had a run of some dreadful decisions in Test cricket in 2000, at a stage when he was desperately trying to get back into form. Twice in the second Test on the Pakistan tour, he found himself given out when he clearly was not, but he showed admirable self-restraint in keeping his bitter disappointment to himself.

Playing Nottinghamshire at Trent Bridge in the 2000 championship, we appealed for a leg before against Jason Gallian when he was on 19. It looked plum but the umpire, Nigel Cowley, a former Glamorgan team-mate of mine, ruled not out. Gallian went on to score a century which effectively won the match for his side at a crucial time of the season: if we had picked up the points for winning, we would virtually have assured ourselves of promotion. Cowley later saw a replay of the incident on video and apologised to me for making the wrong decision. I said there was no need to say sorry, but to try to make sure that it didn't happen again.

Umpiring decisions are subjective and the move towards video technology is positive. Some of the former players of a long time ago are not keen on it, but they belong to a different era when to challenge authority in any walk of life was rare. It is a different age now and if the game has the means to allow umpires to be sure when it comes to tight decisions, those means should be used. But even countless television replays leave room for doubt when it comes to bat-pad appeals or lbws – in which case the benefit of the doubt should be given to the batsman.

Players have to respect the decisions of umpires. What goes around comes around: there are times as a batsman when you suspect you have hit the ball and you are given not out. Cricket is not a black-and-white game and there will always be areas of doubt. And while cameras proliferate at Test matches, they never will do in the county game which will continue to rely on trust between players and umpires.

Which is another reason why I regret the passing of the days when players from both sides used to meet after a day's play to chew things over and the umpires were there as well. We got to know each other properly, whereas now you tend to know someone by reputation. Not all tradition is bad.

17. LORD'S FOR A DAY

I was fast asleep in my hotel room in Brighton in June 2000 when the telephone rang. It was 7.45 a.m. and I thought it was one of the players enjoying his idea of a joke. I thought about letting the phone ring, but eventually picked it up.

'Hello, Matthew, it's Cowdrey here.'

I immediately thought of Chris Cowdrey, the former Kent and England captain who had played for Glamorgan in 1992.

'How are you, Cow?' I mumbled, letting a few early morning pleasantries rip.

I'd got the wrong member of the family: it was Lord Cowdrey of Tonbridge, Chris's father and one of the most eminent men in world, not just British, cricket. He had called to wish me and the team good luck against Gloucestershire in the final of the Benson & Hedges Cup the following weekend and congratulated me on the century I had scored in the semi-final victory over Surrey in Cardiff. Of all the goodwill messages the club received before our first one-day final for 23 years, it was the one I most cherished.

Lord Cowdrey had not only gone to the trouble of finding out where we were playing and in which hotel we were staying, but he had timed his call at a moment when he knew I'd be in my room. I had met him socially on a number of occasions with England and Glamorgan; when he died in December 2000 the game of cricket lost one of its greatest sons. One of the qualities which impressed me about him was that, despite his feats as a player, he was not one to keep referring back to his day. He accepted that cricket had to evolve and that it was a case of adapting to change rather than opposing it as a matter of principle.

We could have done with Lord Cowdrey in his prime in Brighton where we lost heavily to Sussex, both eyes on Lord's. Making a one-day final had long been an ambition of mine and I had fallen at the semi-final hurdle four times: the first occasion, against Derbyshire in the Benson & Hedges Cup semi-final in 1988, provided me with one of the most humiliating moments of my career. I had scored two centuries on our way to the last four as well as 71 against Somerset in a season which was to end with my first England cap and the award of Young Cricketer of the Year.

Hugh Morris won the toss against Derbyshire at St Helen's and put them in. We did well to restrict them to 217 for 8 in their 55 overs, with Steve Barwick and John Derrick each taking three wickets, while Rodney Ontong bowled 11 tight overs of off-spin, conceding a mere 19 runs. We fancied our chances of knocking off the runs, even though rain meant that play had to go into a second day.

Derbyshire's most dangerous bowler was the West Indian Michael Holding whose nickname was 'Whispering Death' because of the way he glided in his run-up before sending down venomous deliveries. He never said anything to a batsman, no matter if there was a lot of playing and missing or thick edges which flew between the slips. He did not have to because he knew, more often than not, he would eventually get his quarry.

I went in first-wicket down after Alan Butcher and John Hopkins had got us off to a solid start, putting on 58 for the first wicket and surviving Holding's first spell. Peter Bowler, an occasional off-spinner, bowled John and the 1 for 15 he took in his three overs that day remains his best figures in the competition. It was an inspired change by the Derbyshire captain, Kim Barnett, and we quickly found ourselves 83 for 3.

I had reached 22 and was feeling confident, playing some forcing shots off the back foot. I had faced Holding in the Sunday League when he had operated with three third men and nobody sweeping in front of the wicket. As a team, we failed to work out a way of playing him and kept trying to drive when the ball was not there for the shot. That was one of the differences Duncan Fletcher made when he took over as coach: he liked nothing better than to work out a batsman or a bowler.

I used to wear a strapless helmet in those days and, as I went back to Holding, my shoulder clipped the ear-piece hanging down from the helmet which fell from my head. I turned round to see the helmet bounce, in slow motion, towards my stumps. There was a full house at Swansea watching with me. I thought, for a hopeful moment, that it was going to roll to safety but it made contact with the off stump and I was on my way. Holding missed the dismissal, having turned to walk back to his mark, stopping only when he heard the celebrations of his team-mates.

We eventually lost by 14 runs and I remain convinced that my helmet cost us a place in the final against Hampshire. When we lost in the NatWest Trophy semi-final against Essex in 1997 after being beaten by Sussex at the same stage in 1993 and by Warwickshire in 1995, I was beginning to think that I was cursed, like a footballer who achieves everything but a day at Wembley in a cup final.

At the start of the 2000 campaign, my priority was winning promotion to the first division of the championship. Deep down, I did not fancy us highly as a one-day side. Our overseas player, Matt Elliott, was a batsman more suited to the four-day game; and whereas in 1993 we had had the ability to strangle the life out of opponents in the field, we no longer had a rigid strategy for limited-overs cricket.

The Benson & Hedges Cup was reintroduced for the 2000 season and it started in the middle of April when the weather was dreadful. We defeated Gloucestershire in a group match in Cardiff, which was reduced to 25 overs a side because of the rain, Steve James and Keith Newell hitting vital runs for us in the middle order. I was criticised during the season for not opening with Sid (that was his usual position in the championship) and opting instead for Robert Croft as a pinch-hitter. But I wanted Sid to be in near the close of an innings because of his ability to run singles quickly. Contrary to popular opinion, the bulk of one-day matches are not won by the team which hits the most boundaries, but by the one which nicks the most singles. Neither Matt Elliott nor Crofty were the most fleet of foot between the wickets, but they could both hit the ball cleanly and score quickly. I felt they were of greater value to us coming in early, leaving the whippets like Sid and Adrian Dale to be at the crease when the need for quick singles was at its most pressing. With only two players allowed outside the circle for the first 15 overs of a one-day game, many sides adopt a pinch-hitter in the hope of getting off to a quick start – and Crofty is under-rated as a batsman.

Later in the season, after Crofty had joined England's one-day squad, I moved Keith Newell up to open and he proved more effective than Crofty. I toyed with the idea of making the move in the final against Gloucestershire, but I told myself not to tinker with what had been a winning format. It was one occasion when I didn't trust my instinct and, in hindsight, I was probably wrong to do so.

We were fortunate to qualify for the knock-out stages of the Benson & Hedges Cup in 2000. We lost heavily at Worcestershire after our opening victory against Gloucestershire, but we had an opportunity to go through to the last eight if we won at Northamptonshire and there was every chance that we would top our group to secure a home draw.

We were sent in to bat on a wicket which looked as if it would offer the bowlers assistance early on, but it was one of the games where Crofty came off. He recognised that we needed a solid, rather than spectacular, start and his presence meant that the opening bowlers tended to bowl short, getting less out of the wicket than they should have done. All our leading batsmen reached double figures and with Sid hitting an unbeaten 33 off 32 balls at the end, we reached 238 for 8 off our 50 overs – a total I was confident our bowlers would defend.

The only batsman to threaten was the Australian international Matthew Hayden, who hit 67 off 72 balls. He swept Crofty for six before the bowler got his revenge the following over with a 23-yard delivery which Hayden was early on: he heard the clatter of his stumps as his gaze fixed on the square-leg boundary. Steve Watkin bowled ten tight overs and Darren Thomas weighed in with three wickets in what was an excellent team performance, our best in one-day cricket for some time.

I left the ground not knowing who we were playing in the quarter-finals or whether we would be home or away. The weather had wreaked such havoc that it was only when all the pool matches had ended that the draw could take place. With so many matches called off in the previous rounds, a team could finish bottom of their pool or top depending on their final result. As I was getting into my car Ian

Botham, who had been commentating on our match for Sky TV, told me that we would be playing Hampshire at Sophia Gardens.

I was delighted because Hampshire had been experiencing batting problems and Len Smith, the groundsman at Sophia Gardens, was having his work cut out trying to produce decent wickets on the square: a marquee had been erected over it the previous autumn for the Rugby World Cup and had rendered the tracks lifeless. Len and his staff did a superb job because by the end of the summer, despite regular cloudbursts, the surface was actually among the best in the championship.

Robin Smith won the toss and put us in. I would have batted, because I knew all about the problems Len had been having. Hampshire bowled accurately and we found ourselves at 83 for 5 off 32 overs. Robin did not appreciate what a decent score was on the wicket and Adrian Dale and Keith Newell, our last two recognised batsmen, were given too many singles as Hampshire looked to keep down the twos and the boundaries. We dealt with Shane Warne well and a stand off 99 for the sixth wicket, broken on the last ball of the innings when Keith was run out going for the second run which would have brought him a richly deserved fifty, took us to 182 for 6 off our 50 overs.

Hampshire only managed four runs off the bat in their first six overs, with Owen Parkin taking two wickets. Steve Watkin returned the remarkable figures of 2 for 3 off seven overs as we bowled them out for 69 to win by 113 runs. Robin publicly criticised the pitch afterwards. He did not blame it for Hampshire's defeat, pointing out that it was equally bad for both sides, but said he was grateful he didn't have to bat on it every week. There were extenuating circumstances, though, and it was not poor by design.

Another semi-final and another match in Cardiff. If Hampshire had batting frailties, Surrey boasted the likes of Mark Butcher, Alec Stewart, Graham Thorpe, Alistair Brown and the Hollioake brothers and batted all the way down. Our plan was to go in first and post a score in excess of 220: with Alan Butcher by now on Surrey's coaching staff, I knew there was little chance that they would put us in if Adam Hollioake won the toss and they had beaten us in a Sunday League match in Cardiff a month before after batting first.

Hollioake called wrong and we batted. Rain had washed out the first five hours of play and the match was bound to go into a second day. We lost both our openers quickly; but Mike Powell started positively, hitting Alex Tudor for three boundaries in four balls, and we put on 133 for the third wicket. Like me at the start of my career, Mike was a player who took to championship cricket quicker than the one-day game, but he came of age in that match. We were 99 for 2 with nearly half of our overs gone when rain finally ended play on the first day.

I was on 34 and went to a pub near Sophia Gardens with some friends of mine who had come down from North Wales for the match. I only had a couple of shandies. Although a number of supporters commented that I should be back home in bed rather than supping beer, it was my way of relaxing and putting the following day to the back of my mind for a while. Mike went on to make 67, while I reached my century off 109 balls with a four off Martin Bicknell. I was out for 109 with the score on 226 for 4 and the one disappointment about our innings was that we slumped to 251 and did not use up our full allocation of overs. There were four run-outs and an air of panic which suggested that our semi-final curse had not breathed its last.

Two wickets in two balls in Owen Parkin's third over calmed us. The dangerous Brown was brilliantly caught by Matt Elliott before Alex Tudor was trapped leg before. I felt we were always in charge after that and at 125 for 7, with only 17 overs to go, the game looked up for Surrey. But Stewart was anchoring one end while Jason Ratcliffe and then Martin Bicknell blazed away at the other, and 41 runs off five overs gave Surrey hope – until Parky took the final two wickets.

The crucial spell for us had been bowled by Alex Wharf. Graham Thorpe had settled in with Stewart before I, on a whim, brought Alex back into the attack. He beat Thorpe for pace with his first ball and removed the Hollioake brothers in his next two overs: worth every month of his three-year contract. I always prefer to play Surrey when they have their England players on duty because they seem to have less hunger about them. The semi-final was definitely an occasion when we wanted it more than them.

It took some while before the realisation sank in that we were going to Lord's. The fact that we were playing Gloucestershire, who had won both the one-day knock-out tournaments the previous year, sobered everyone up. The delight at making it to the final was tempered by the appreciation that we were not going to London for a day out, but to *win*, and that meant getting the better of the best limited overs side in the country.

Everyone was counting down to the day and our championship form deteriorated. Whereas we normally travelled to away matches by car, we booked a coach to take us to London. This was due to pick us up at Sophia Gardens at 9 a.m. on the day before the match to take us to our hotel opposite the Lord's ground. It was 11.30 a.m. before the driver turned up – not the ideal start to the weekend, with players pacing around nervously with nothing to do and nowhere to go while the club's cricket secretary, Caryl Watkin, frantically tried to find out what had happened to the bus. We'd booked the nets at Lord's for two hours after 2 p.m., with Gloucestershire arriving at 4 p.m., and we missed our first hour because of the coach company's mistake: as it was raining, we had to go indoors.

St John's Wood reverberated to the sound of Welsh accents on the Friday and the Saturday. I have been back to Lord's a few times since the final and everyone I've spoken to at the ground has remarked on the atmosphere generated by our supporters. I went out for a drink on the eve of the match with Mike Fatkin, Duncan Fletcher and Dean Conway. I had a half in the team hotel, but supporters and members of the committee kept giving me dirty looks and I wanted to go somewhere to relax and enjoy the evening. We found a pub nearer the centre of London and I sank two or three pints – in bed by 10 p.m., though.

Next day, I won the toss and batted. Ian Harvey removed Crofty and Matt Elliott in his first five overs, leaving Mike Powell and me together with the score on 24 for 2. Mike was tense and Mike Smith sensed his anxiety by calling for a short leg. Gradually, he relaxed and started letting the ball come on to his bat. The runs started to come and we pushed Gloucestershire on to the defensive. I had started quietly, content to push the singles, before finding my stride. The crowd was unlike anything I had ever experienced at a cricket match: when I reached my half-century our supporters started singing 'Hymns and Arias' and I had to compose myself for a couple of deliveries, overcome by emotion.

Mike and I put on 137 for the third wicket before he was deceived by the off-spinner Jeremy Snape into offering a return catch: 161 for 3. With ten overs to go we should have been looking at a score of around 250, but Gloucestershire are at their most dangerous when they scent blood. They kept me away from the strike and, though I was the last man out, I was only to receive another 22 deliveries. They applied the pressure and the wickets tumbled.

I reached my century with four overs to go. Mark Alleyne, the Gloucestershire captain, shook my hand and was followed by all of his players, a gesture which summed up the side. We closed on 225, below par for the wicket, but a total we had the ability to defend. It needed our opening bowlers to find their line immediately, but both Owen Parkin and Steve Watkin were guilty of trying too hard on the big day. Watty gripped the ball so hard that he sent down a couple of long hops, something I had very rarely seen him do. Gloucestershire had 50 on the board before the end of the ninth over, with Tim Hancock and Kim Barnett punishing anything remotely off line.

Crofty ended the stand when he bowled Barnett, before Parky and Watty struck in their second spells. At 131 for 3, with 20 overs to go, we were back in with a chance. We had an early lbw shout against Mark Alleyne turned down and Matt Windows chipped one shot just over my head. Small margins again: the pair remained to take Gloucestershire to a deserved success by seven wickets. We had been outplayed, but not disgraced as we had been by the same opponents in Cardiff the year before.

I was made the man of the match in a presentation ceremony which had 'Made in Wales' stamped all over it. Tony Lewis was the president of the MCC and Duncan Fletcher presented the man-of-the-match award while David Morgan, who had taken over as the Glamorgan chairman from Tony Lewis, presented the trophy to Mark Alleyne. David had been the chairman for five years and was a rare breed of committeeman, someone who offered his support after a bad defeat or a low score. He would always have a chat with Sue or Mum when walking round the outfield and he was a big loss to the county when he stood down. I might not have much time for committees, but guys like David Morgan are worth their weight in gold.

I was made the man of the match for my 104, but the match-winner had been Ian Harvey with his five wickets. I am not sure what I have done with the trophy I was presented with, but the cash went into the players' kitty. After I have retired I will find that trophy and perhaps put it on display in my house; however, the defeat still hurts and my award is a reminder of that. The occasion was without any doubt worth the wait, but for weeks afterwards I was playing various incidents in the match in my mind: if only, what if . . . ?

We sat in the dressing-room for what seemed hours afterwards. The empty feeling that defeat brings takes more than a few drinks afterwards to fill. We had been beaten by a better team, but that did not make the pain any less acute. I thought of our magnificent supporters. St John's Wood had become little Wales for the weekend and, to a man, we were determined to make it to another final for our fans. They had deserved better.

Glamorgan put on a function for the players in our hotel on the Saturday evening. I made a short speech, but I can't remember what I said. I remember the barman saying I couldn't have any more Jack Daniels because he had run dry and Sue saying that it was time to call it a day. The highs and the lows: there are occasions when you have to deal with the twin impostors at virtually the same time, but not even experience helps you deal with failure.

There was always the NatWest Trophy. It was back to Canterbury for our first match. Rain held up the start of play and, with the conditions damp, I put Kent into bat. They were soon in trouble with Alex Wharf and Parky striking from the 14th over. Alex took his three wickets in a 14-ball spell as Kent slumped from 32 for no wicket to 66 for 6 with only Paul Nixon standing firm as we bowled them out for 121.

We closed the day at 65 for 1 after 13 overs, victory seemingly a formality. David Masters, the son of my old mate Kevin, had removed Matt Elliott, but Keith Newell was batting with a flourish. It was like a different match the following morning: Mark Ealham found his mark and tormented us with his swing. He removed Steve James, me, Adrian Dale and Mike Powell in a five-over spell – all caught off edges – while conceding just three runs. At 86 for 5 we were in trouble, fortunate that Newell had survived.

Adrian Shaw, who was having his best season with the bat, provided vital support and we won by five wickets. Our reward was a trip to

Edgbaston to play Warwickshire in the quarter-final. I again fielded first and we had them in trouble when Alex Wharf took wickets in consecutive overs. Nick Knight was dropped when he was on nine and went on to make 118 as they piled up 273 for 7. The total was always beyond us and we lost by 81 runs.

Our one-day form had deserted us at the same time as we had put a good run together in the championship. Our day in Lord's seemed another world away, long gone but not forgotten. Cricket may change, but one thing stays the same: the thrill of playing in a one-day final.

18. ALL IN THE MIND

As I sat in the Lord's dressing-room after the defeat against Gloucestershire, I was joined by Bill Clutterbuck, my batting mentor who had been a big part of my career for 20 years. He used to be the professional at Bangor Cricket Club and part of his duties was to look after the square. I used to cadge a lift from my parents or cycle the eight miles from my Menai Bridge home to spend three afternoons a week with Bill in the summer holidays, helping him with his work on the ground before being given an hour in the nets as a reward.

Before the start of every season, I have spent four or five days with Bill, who is now the head groundsman at Guildford Cricket Club. We spend six or seven hours in the nets each day, refining my technique and preparing for the summer ahead. When I was 14 Dad decided that, having fired my enthusiasm for cricket, he could do no more for me and suggested that I join the Bangor club. It was the first season that they had a professional: the choice was between Bill and the former Glamorgan bowler Tony Cordle.

Bill invested a lot of his time in me, and still does, but before the Gloucestershire game he had never seen me score a century. I have been through a number of lean spells in my career, as happens to every player. Bill has always been on the end of a telephone, though I have never turned to him for reassurance. Batting is very much a battle of the mind and when you go through a period when you don't know where your next run is coming from, self-doubt creeps in and you wonder how you ever made a century.

Bill is quick to spot any technical faults and I would not have achieved anywhere near as much in my career without his guidance. I have also been fortunate at Glamorgan with the likes of Alan Jones, John Steele, Rodney Ontong, John Derrick, Duncan Fletcher and Jeff Hammond. I used to learn a lot from opponents in the days when teams spent some time together after a day's play; and even at this stage, when my career is in its latter stages, I am still learning.

The late Sir Jack Hobbs, in the last season of his long career, said that you never stopped finding out things, about yourself as well as the game. He was right. My biggest help in the Glamorgan dressing-room has been Robert Croft, an all-rounder with a sharp cricketing brain. He sums up players impressively quickly and he should make a successful coach when he retires from playing. He was one of the candidates to succeed me as the Glamorgan captain, along with Steve James and Adrian Dale.

Sid was given the job by the committee – possibly because they saw him as being less confrontational than me, while Crofty never leaves anyone in any doubt as to what he is thinking. Sid is no mouse. He is a quiet man, but he is someone who has always put the team first and his strength of character is shown by some of the big scores he has scored for Glamorgan: 235, 259 and 309. That shows his self-discipline and burning determination. He made the 235 against Nottinghamshire at Worksop and one of the bowlers he plundered was the New Zealand international Chris Cairns. 'How has this guy never played for England?' Cairns asked me after the match, saying that he'd never in his career found a batsman so hard to get out. Because he is self-effacing on the surface, some do see Sid as a soft touch. But they soon learn.

He usually has a ding-dong with the England and Somerset fast bowler Andy Caddick, who is not slow to tell batsmen what he thinks. While I shut up and let bowlers let off steam, Sid often has a go back and he and Caddick have had words on a number of occasions, including at Taunton in 1997 when we only needed 11 to win in our second innings. Caddick steamed in at Sid as if we needed 311, cursing when a couple of appeals were turned down. However he was wasting his breath on a player who, when he first started playing for Glamorgan, was limited in his strokeplay but, through hard work and determination, turned himself into one of the most consistent batsmen in the country. Sid did eventually play for England, but his two caps were scant reward for a player of his ability and courage. I am not sure that the selectors at the time expected him to succeed: he should have been given a whole series with the time to adjust to international cricket.

Crofty has won 17 England caps, the record for a Glamorgan player, but he threw a wobbly after being omitted from the squad which toured Pakistan and Sri Lanka in the 2000–01 winter and said he was considering retiring from international cricket. He was pilloried in the media, where it was said that, given his lack of wickets in his last few matches for England, he would have been fortunate to have been chosen again.

That was an unfair and, in some cases, a churlish reaction. Very few commentators pointed out that the lot of a finger-spinner on British wickets is not a happy one. We seem to be the only country in the world where bad wickets are prepared deliberately and it is an issue the England and Wales Cricket Board must look at closely in the coming years. The question has to be asked: where are the young flair batsmen? When Andrew Flintoff started making a name for himself with some Bothamesque innings, he was pilloried for being an overweight slogger.

'Not bad for a fat lad,' he said memorably after a match-winning innings for England in a one-dayer, and talents like Flintoff's should be nurtured and enhanced. Instead he gets knocked and we are in danger of producing cricketers who are broadly similar in terms of technique and temperament. Teams need a Gower as much as they require a Boycott, but county wickets are encouraging orthodoxy by making strokeplay hazardous, just as they reward ordinary medium-pacers more than spinners.

I would like to see the England and Wales Cricket Board centrally contracting every groundsman in the first-class game. Captains and coaches would not then be able to demand that a certain pitch be produced. The groundsmen, and the board, would be in control. When we played Gloucestershire at Bristol last year, the wicket was not designed for a four-day match and we suffered a heavy defeat. Not long afterwards the Gloucestershire coach, John Bracewell, attacked the standard of wickets in the championship, but his county had not been averse from joining the rush for mediocrity when it suited them: they were without their leading seamers against us and struggling near the foot of the division, while we had won four matches in a row. The wicket made the game a lottery and there was no telling who would come up with the winning ticket.

Those who criticise Crofty with such vehemence should look at the broader picture: the decline of British finger spinners. It was heartening to see Ashley Giles doing well on the Pakistan tour, but he was bowling on wickets which suited the slower bowlers. When Glamorgan played the West Indians in the summer of 2000, Crofty took 5 for 26 in their first innings and 3 for 44 in the second. The wicket helped him, but he had all their batsmen in trouble and carefully thought them out. It earned him a recall to the England side and the scene was set for him at Old Trafford in the West Indies' second innings with the wicket expected to turn and England bowling for victory.

In the event he only took one wicket and that was taken as evidence that he wasn't up to it at Test level. He bowled as well as he did against the West Indians in Cardiff, beating the bat on numerous occasions, but whereas before he had got the edge, this time the millimetres were against him. I was not surprised when he was recalled to the England squad for the tour of Sri Lanka early in 2001. He turned 30 in 2000 – no age for a spinner – and if there are times when he needs to count to ten, particularly when it comes to the England selectors, his attitude is certainly more healthy than mine was. I bottled everything up inside and I suffered for it. At least Crofty will never be left wondering why.

I would expect Crofty to be the Glamorgan captain when Sid decides to stand down. They are different characters on the surface, but they are both Glamorgan players to the core. Sid was born in Gloucestershire, but has spent his first-class career in Wales and is regarded as a native son. Crofty wears his Welshness on his sleeve. They have both had the strength of character to overcome adversity: Sid refined his batting technique after sides quickly rumbled him as a player who compiled his runs behind square; Crofty found himself subjected to a bouncer ordeal by Australia.

The Aussies had identified that he had a flawed technique against the short delivery and, for a player who had scored centuries at county level, he was made to look like a tail-ender – hopelessly deficient when the ball was speared in at his body at pace. Crofty's answer was to spend weeks travelling up the M4 and the M25 to work with Graham Gooch at Essex. Some had seen the problem as a lack of courage, because he was struggling to get in line, but really it had nothing to do with bottle as Crofty, with Gooch's help, has since shown.

Cricket can often be a battle as much with your own mind as with the opposition, and it is often cruel. You can spend a couple of days in the field watching batsmen plunder runs and then get a faint edge first ball and miss out on a belter. I had a dreadful period with the bat in the middle of the 2000 season after my Benson & Hedges Cup final century: the initial problem was one of attitude after being overlooked by England, but by the time I had pulled myself together mentally I was locked in a run of low scores. They say that form is temporary while class is permanent, and batting can be different from one session to the next let alone one day, one week or one month: many's the time I have gone in for lunch or tea feeling on top of the bowling, only to find myself on the back foot when play resumes.

Some have argued that batting for England became a mental problem for me and it must have looked that way when I played in the 2000 triangular tournament against Sri Lanka and West Indies. Left out of the original squad, I was brought in when Nasser Hussain broke his finger and played in four matches, batting only in the first two. I made three and a duck: bowled trying to hit the leg-spinner Paul Strang over the top against Zimbabwe, before returning to Lord's to face West Indies and being dismissed when I left a delivery from Cory Collymore which nipped back up the slope and bowled me.

The dismissals did look bad. Against Zimbabwe we had just been off for rain and Strang floated one up over the sightscreen. Perhaps I lost it for a second, but it looked to be there to hit and as I walked off the field I saw the replay on the video screen and felt a fool because the ball was there to be put away. I felt more hard done by against West Indies: the wicket was green and there seemed no point in chasing Collymore's wide delivery before I had got my eye in.

I could not believe it when the ball defied the law of Lord's, where balls usually move down the slope, and I trudged off forlornly wondering if I would ever enjoy some fortune batting for England. Alec Stewart sympathised with me in the dressing-room, saying it had not been a bad leave. We won the next two matches with ease and I was not needed to bat. By the time it came for the finals against Zimbabwe, Nasser was fit again and I returned to Glamorgan.

I knew that my only chance of making the winter tour was if Gulliver's offered me another job as a guide, but I had thought my England career had long ended. When I failed to make the winter tour in 1997, which in my view was my best-ever season for Glamorgan, my international career was all but over. I had had my chance, more than one, and it will always be a source of regret and frustration that I will be judged a failure at Test level – more proof that all that glitters is not gold.

I was not the player England needed in 1988 or 1993 because that was an era when you had to put yourself before the team, when the pain of losing was less if you had scored runs and taken wickets and therefore justified your place. Graham Thorpe had been, I felt, a player who became obsessed with his own performances to the point where the team became subservient to the individual, but to be with him in the triangular series was to see a new man. He applauded as enthusiastically as anyone even when he had not been required to bat. The Thorpe of old had been the product of an age where failure did not often meet with a second chance. You needed to be driven by a burning inner desire and I have never been someone who has been dominated by ambition. It was never a burning ambition of mine when I was a boy to become a professional sportsman. When I did sign for Glamorgan, playing for England did not enter my thinking. As a fatalist, I take what comes: if it is meant to be, it will be.

Success, like wealth, is relative. Brian Lara is regarded by many as the greatest batsman in the world today, but since his 375 against England in 1994 his career has taken several detours and even he appears to have been wracked by self-doubt on occasions. Australia are the best team in the world because they are strong mentally: they apply equal pressure with the bat and the ball and I admire their attitude because they give players a chance to prove themselves. West Indies were the major force in the 1980s, especially under Viv Richards, a player who exuded menace and confidence – but even Viv had his moments when he could not impose himself.

Cricket is a game where you can be horribly exposed and Crofty felt the pressure when he returned to Glamorgan after his experience at Old Trafford. He had been expected to bowl West Indies out: in a sense he had been playing for his Test place and the pressure showed. When former Glamorgan players, like Tony Cottey and David Hemp, batted against us I always used to get Crofty on quickly because he knows how to get them out: when Hemp came to the wicket at 148 for 3 in the NatWest Trophy tie at Edgbaston in the 2000 season, Crofty dismissed him first ball, not for the first time.

That's one reason why I rate him highly as a player and why I believe those who argue that Crofty's international days are over are wrong. A lot will depend on how he does for Glamorgan, but if the England and Wales Cricket Board would start treating spinners as a protected species and doing everything in their power to ensure that they not only survive but also grow in number, it would enhance the championship as well as the England side.

The one big difference between the game today and when I made my first-class début in 1985 is the lack of real variety in the modern game. That is why I think Crofty will make an excellent coach: he reads situations well and keeps thinking. You have to emphasise the natural. I have been cursed by our supporters and rebuked in the media for playing one attacking shot too many, but you can only play as you are, not as someone wants you to be. Dad taught me that lesson early on; and while he would talk to me about technical matters such as my stance and the straightness of my bat, he never criticised my attacking inclination, any more than he would have complained if I had been a defensive batsman. All he wanted to ensure was that I had the tools to maximise my effectiveness and that is why my relationship with Bill Clutterbuck has been so strong.

It is not about letting alone balls which pass invitingly by my off stump, but working on the foundation of my game such as stance and pick-up – oiling the engine rather than overhauling it. That, to me, is what coaching should be all about. At the end of the day, and it does not matter if you are an amateur or a professional, sport is about enjoyment. If you try to be what you are not, or someone forces you to defy your instincts, there can be no ultimate fulfilment, no enjoyment.

I was the same player who made a century at Lord's the one month and a duck the next. There was a large crowd on both occasions, so it could hardly have been a question of bottling it in the one-day international. I will always back myself to score runs when it matters, but cricket, like life, has a habit of bringing you down. For every hundred there is a duck.

19. THREE INTO TWO MUST STAY

I had opposed the move to split the championship into two divisions and Glamorgan were the only county to vote against the change. I felt that the act smacked of desperation after England's continued failure with the England and Wales Cricket Board looking at the county set-up rather than the national side itself. The board were astute in getting the counties to agree to the move to restructure the championship before proposing to contract a number of leading players centrally.

Had the Board tried to push through the two-division reform after getting counties to agree to central contracts, I am sure they would have met with stiffer opposition because sides would have realised that they faced losing key players for crucial matches, with relegation and promotion an issue. I have long been a supporter of central contracts because they give the England coach more control of his own destiny: he can rest players as he sees fit and ensure they are raring to go for Test matches.

The flip side – as counties like Yorkshire and Somerset found out in the 2000 season when they were without Darren Gough and Andy Caddick respectively for a number of matches – is that the championship can be devalued, with members of counties asking if they are being short-changed by rarely seeing their sides at full strength. If the championship had remained as it was, without the spectre of relegation and the commercial threat to counties that it poses, the board would have been able to contract 25 players rather than less than half that number.

I was wrong about the split into divisions in the sense that, in the second division at least, the 2000 season was tense and exciting with the final two promotion places only decided in the final session of the last round of matches: Northamptonshire had earlier ensured they would finish top. The first division was more clear cut with Durham, Hampshire and Derbyshire occupying the bottom three places for most of the season, while Surrey never looked like being overhauled as champions.

When I was made the captain of Glamorgan, my dream was to lead the county into the new millennium. I only just made it, but I was glad that I did. Jeff Hammond, the former Australian Test bowler, had taken over as our coach from Duncan Fletcher, after Hansie Cronje and Greg Chappell had turned the job down. He was a totally different character to Fletch, more outgoing and less organised. I did not develop the same close relationship with him that I'd had with Fletch, but I did not make any attempt to do so because I knew it was going to be my last season in charge.

Jeff had to reinvent himself as a cricketer after a serious back injury ended his career as a fast bowler. He became an opening batsman, good enough to play at state level, and he brought an infectious enthusiasm for the game with him to Glamorgan. He did a lot of excellent work with the bowlers – although, to me, he was a less effective batting coach and lacked Fletch's organisational skills – and he had an influence in what was a successful season for us because we improved without question as a bowling side in both forms of cricket.

I received a lot of the credit for the fact we got to Lord's because of my century against Surrey, but I always felt that the bowlers got us there with their ability to defend totals and take wickets at crucial times. The fact they could not repeat that form against Gloucestershire in no way detracted from their contribution and they rarely let us down in the championship. Jeff did an excellent job with them.

When we lost to Sussex at Hove at the beginning of June – hammered by ten wickets in a match when we couldn't have played worse if we'd tried – we slumped to the bottom of the championship. A reporter asked me whether I felt our promotion chances had already died. I replied that, with teams bound to be more conservative with more at stake than ever before, and less inclined to make sporting declarations, I felt it would be a season when a team would rocket up the table if it put together a winning run.

And so it proved. We went from the bottom to the top in a month after four straight victories, our best run for 31 years, and so did Northamptonshire. They looked anything but potential winners of the division when we completed the double over them at Sophia Gardens in July, but they never looked back after that. Gloucestershire very nearly came back from the dead: marooned at the bottom, they put together an impressive run and only just missed out on promotion.

We had been a Jekyll-and-Hyde side in 1999, losing four matches by an innings and winning two in the same fashion. The second division looked as strong as the first, with sides like Warwickshire, Essex and Middlesex all winning the championship during the 1990s. Meanwhile Nottinghamshire had shown their intentions by signing the Pakistan fast bowler Shoaib Akhtar. Unfortunately for them, injury meant that Akhtar was forced to stay at home, though his bowling action was by then under close scrutiny by the authorities.

Batting was our main problem throughout the season. We achieved maximum batting points in our second match (at Warwickshire), something we were not to do again until August, and we had to wait for the end of June for our first victory (against Worcestershire, at St Helen's). The key matches were away to Northamptonshire and Middlesex in July: I missed them because I was with the England one-day squad and Steve James, my vice-captain, took over.

We won them both and I think the successes persuaded Sid that he would be suited to the captaincy. I was travelling to a match in the car with him in August and he raised the subject of the captaincy. He was concerned at the greater scrutiny he would come under, especially in the media, and wondered if he would be as thick-skinned as I when it came to criticism.

I have never worried about what anyone says or writes about me. If a commentator thinks I am not good enough to play for England, fair enough. It is his opinion, not a fact, and if sport is all about diversity then so is the coverage of it. I have never taken criticism of me personally, no matter how strident it may have been. There is no point in letting it get you down. If you have the confidence in your own ability, it does not matter what anyone says about you. And at the end of the day, it is not up to the critics: they don't go out to bat for you or take your place in the field. Players have the real power over the media, because we are the ones who can perform and decide our own destinies.

Cricket has a fair coverage overall. It is unique among the major team sports because, certainly in the championship, it does not have a major spectator base. How many supporters can afford to take one day off, let alone four, to watch a championship match? The sparse crowds have been taken by some as evidence of cricket's decline – but the championship game is one which by nature is more read about than watched, and the broadsheet newspapers do a thorough job in covering it. My fear about two-division cricket is that the coverage will concentrate on the first division, to the detriment of the second division which will become second class. That must not be allowed to happen.

Sid was concerned about the media, which surprised me slightly because in the winter he covers rugby matches for a national Sunday newspaper. Opinions are what sport, what life, is all about, no matter how irrational or misguided they may seem. Players should not need to look to the media for reassurance: it should come from within. There are times when you get it wrong, as I have done many times as a player and as a captain. When that has happened, I've always believed in facing the media rather than trying to hide away, because they act as the link between players and supporters. Fans are entitled, after all, to know why you made a certain decision as a captain or played what looked like an unwise shot as a batsman.

So much happens on a cricket field which is not always apparent to those who are watching from the boundary, and that applies to the members of the batting side who are in the pavilion. I have always believed in keeping the media informed. If someone has had a go at me, I immediately forget about it. If you let criticism get to you, it can have a cancerous effect. It is a question of letting it ride over you. I'm not sure that I really have a thick skin, merely a desire to succeed, and I know when I have performed inadequately.

Sid should have no problems. Anyone who can make 309, as he did for us against Sussex at Colwyn Bay in August 2000, has a stronger character than most. For the second year in a row, we made our highest first-class score: 718 for 3 declared against Sussex topped the 648 for 4 we had made against Nottinghamshire the previous year at the same ground. Sid had made an unbeaten 259 in that match, just 28 short of the club record set by Emrys Davies in 1939, and he wondered if he would have the chance to get near it again.

Colwyn Bay has become a lucky ground for us, much to my delight because it is near my old stamping grounds in north Wales. The five days we spend there gives me the chance to catch up with old friends. Since Glamorgan bought Sophia Gardens in the 1990s, we have played the bulk of our home matches there (whereas before we used to take the game around), but the local authority in Colwyn Bay make it worth the club's while to take a championship and a Sunday League fixture there and, from a player's point of view, it is one of the most popular weeks of the season.

Too popular in 1997 for Phil North, my former Glamorgan team-mate, who would have won a championship medal in 1997 but for a late night. Phil had been released by the club in 1989 – harshly, in my view, because he was the best of the slow left armers we had on our books then. He was playing league and Minor Counties cricket and I called him into the squad for the match against Nottinghamshire in north Wales because one of our spinners, Dean Cosker, was playing in an Under-19 Test for England.

The first day was washed out and we hired a minibus to go to a pub in Conwy called the Liverpool Arms. Phil is a raconteur and amused everyone with his fund of stories and anecdotes, but we did not make a night of it and were back in our hotel by 9 p.m. Phil, though, had got himself into a social mood and ended up in a nightclub, while his room-mate, Hugh Morris, got an early night. Phil was early, too: early in the morning.

Hugh had a face like thunder at breakfast and I asked him what had happened. 'That mate of yours,' he said, 'not only pitched up at 2.30 in the morning, but turned on the television, smoked a fag, fell asleep and snored all night. I've had hardly any sleep.' Hugh had every right to feel angry and Phil had broken the cardinal rule of room-sharing. It was no surprise when he failed to turn up for breakfast and I expected to see him at the ground.

He had driven up to Colwyn Bay on his own, having been

summoned late, but by the time all the players had got to the ground and changed there was no sign of Phil. The rule was that players had to be ready for training by 9.15 a.m. Phil finally made it at 10.30 a.m., having slept through his alarm and a nudge from Hugh. The start of play had been delayed, so I'd not had to hand in my team-sheet to the umpires, but there was no way I could tell Gary Butcher, a contracted player, that he was twelfth man while Phil took the field. Good mate or not, Phil had to go back to Cardiff with a tale to tell, but with no chance of a championship medal. I was at a barbecue a couple of weeks later when Phil turned up with a huge alarm clock draped around his neck. We could laugh about it then, but the lack of a second spinner at Colwyn Bay that year could have cost us the title because we failed to winkle out the Nottinghamshire tail-enders.

The Sussex match in 2000 in a sense summed up our championship campaign because, after Sid, Matt Elliott and Mike Powell had all scored centuries, we still had to bowl out Sussex twice on a flat track. Alex Wharf, Steve Watkin, Adrian Dale and Darren Thomas all made inroads and the victory put us back into the promotion frame after we had slipped down the table. We had gone to the top after our run of four successive victories: at Southgate against Middlesex and at home to Northamptonshire, we had successfully chased a target in excess of 300 in the fourth innings with Matt getting a century in each match.

It justified the decision to sign Matt as our overseas player and it was a big blow to us when a knee injury forced him to return home to Australia with three matches still to play. With the promotion race so tight, my concern was that his absence could make the difference between going up or just missing out. I was cursing my fortune, because in my five years as captain I had only once had my overseas player for an entire season: Waqar Younis in 1997. There were some rumblings that Matt was hamming the injury up because he had just got back into the Australian squad and they were about to go into a training camp, but he was not that sort of man.

He was as determined as anyone to achieve promotion and it turned out, when he returned home, that the injury was a serious one. He played his part in our success that season: a batsman who priced his wicket highly and a dextrous, supple fielder who was like a praying mantis in the slips or at short mid-wicket. He was typically Australian in his attitude, but he also knew how to enjoy himself and I have still not managed to work out how he scored 88 in a Sunday League match against Derbyshire the day after we'd beaten Surrey in the Benson & Hedges Cup semi-final – he was nursing the mother of all hangovers, after a celebration which went on a bit, and only missed out on his century after running himself out.

As one door closed, another opened. Matt's departure meant a promotion for another left-handed opener, Ian Thomas. Ian had started the season as a fringe Second XI player, but a series of big scores gave him his chance and he made 82 at Southend coming in at number eight before partnering Steve James at the top of the order for the final two matches.

It was a season which twisted and turned. After our winning streak we had matches against Gloucestershire and Nottinghamshire, two teams struggling near the foot of the division. We were well beaten at Bristol, on a surface which was comfortably the worst I played on all summer, and then had the worst of a draw against Nottinghamshire in Cardiff. It was essential that we defeated Sussex and we ended up being promoted, even though we did not win any of our final three matches.

We should have beaten Essex, one of our promotion rivals, at Southend. We scored 507, bowled them out for 292 and reduced them to 53 for 3 in their second innings, only for nightwatchman Ashley Cowan to add 146 for the fourth wicket with Stuart Law. Ronnie Irani, who had a superb year for Essex and who had scored 95 in the first innings, frustrated us again and we had to settle for a draw. Injuries and a poor umpiring decision cost us at Trent Bridge and we went into our final match against Middlesex not knowing what we needed to do to win promotion.

Six sides were vying for the two remaining promotion places: Essex and Warwickshire were playing each other, as were Gloucestershire and Nottinghamshire. Worcestershire were at home to Northamptonshire while we had our jinx team, Middlesex. They, together with Sussex, were the only ones in the division without a chance of being promoted. Their only aim was to avoid finishing bottom of the championship for the first time in their history.

For once, the weather worked in our favour. It rained in Cardiff, it poured down in Worcester and Bristol and they even had a drop of the wet stuff in Chelmsford. The weather meant that none of our rivals could achieve maximum bonus points and a victory: they had to go for one or the other and what it boiled down to, on the final day of the season, was that if we got our three bowling points against Middlesex and drew, only the winner of the match between Essex and Warwickshire could overtake us. With three going up, that did not matter.

We had made 325 in our first innings, 25 runs short of a fourth batting point, having been 257 for 5. Mike Powell batted superbly for his 114: he timed the ball as well as anyone I had seen all year. With Adrian Dale and Robert Croft making half-centuries, I was not unhappy with the score, especially when we had Middlesex at 40 for 4 with Owen Parkin taking all the wickets. A day to get five wickets against the bottom club. A formality, surely?

Glamorgan, however, would not be Glamorgan without twists and turns. Middlesex's leading batsmen, Justin Langer and Mark Ramprakash, were at the crease and they had both enjoyed successful summers individually. Langer, the Australian Test player, was the Middlesex captain, but I hadn't talked to him at all during the game about contriving a finish. My fear that day was that once he had got to 250 and achieved the second batting point which condemned Sussex to bottom place, he would declare. That would have left us with no chance of winning and put us in danger of not going up unless we'd taken nine wickets.

Langer and Ramprakash had added 94 for the fifth wicket. Then Darren Thomas removed the latter. Darren should not have played in the match, because he had a persistent groin strain. He insisted, though – which, considering the disappointment he had felt after being overlooked for the Benson & Hedges Cup final, showed again what a huge heart he had. He pounded in all day, despite the discomfort he was in, and he was to get his reward. Langer, who had been dropped the previous evening, was having one of those days when everything found the middle of his bat. I could not see us getting him out and concentrated on the other end. David Nash was proving an obdurate foil for his skipper and at 221 for 5, with less than ten minutes to go before lunch, we desperately needed a wicket. Two of the other three matches affecting us were being played to a finish.

I decided to bring on Keith Newell for an over. I don't know why. I had been rotating the quicker bowlers and Crofty without any joy. Newell was the sort of bowler who broke stands, often tempting batsmen to have a go at him before getting used to his pace. Nash had a go at Keith's second delivery, but failed to keep the ball down and Mike Powell took a super catch at extra cover. Three wickets and one more point to go.

Richard Johnson joined Langer and the pair earned Middlesex their second batting point. Langer turned to me and asked how I saw the game going. 'Carry on batting,' I told him, but at 302 for 6 we were feeling the tension. Then Darren, straining every sinew, bowled Johnson a pearler which seamed, lifted and found the edge to give Mike Powell a catch at slip. Gus Fraser did not hang around, chipping Crofty to backward square leg: 323 for 8 and we were almost there.

Fittingly, Darren bagged the wicket which took us into the first division, Tim Bloomfield edging a catch to Mark Wallace. And we were there, bar a batting collapse on the lines of Middlesex at Cardiff in 1997. It did not matter what happened elsewhere and we could relax and marvel at Langer, who finished unbeaten on 213. Essex defeated Warwickshire, after being set a generous target, to finish second in the table. We ended up third and there were mutterings during the season that three up and three down was ludicrous for two divisions of just nine teams. There will be pressure to reduce it to two or even one in the next few seasons. That must be resisted, otherwise the first division will simply become a league apart.

Warwickshire's failure to go up cost Neil Smith his job as captain. Never mind that they had made the NatWest Trophy final, only for the Duckworth-Lewis method to cost them victory against Gloucestershire! Warwickshire, like Nottinghamshire, paid a price for having very good wickets on which it was difficult to bowl sides out twice: we made 400 at Edgbaston and were forced to follow on. They both drew games while other sides, who had prepared result tracks, were either winning or losing.

The following day we lost to Middlesex in the Sunday League off the last ball, which meant we would have to play a first-class county in the first round proper of the following season's major one-day knock-out competition. NatWest had withdrawn as sponsors and the England

and Wales Cricket Board were seeking new backers. Yet with just a small swing in our favour, we would have achieved promotion in the Sunday League.

Six of our matches went down to the last over, and we failed in most of them. Too often, the main batsman lost the strike and could not get it back. The championship was our priority, but it meant we had not done badly in any of the four competitions we played in. We were competitive again and we were in the first division. At least I was bowing out as captain on a high: had I gone in 1999, it would have been an anti-climax.

I negotiated a new three-year deal with Glamorgan which I expect to be my last as a player. When I was going through the contract with the club's chief executive, Mike Fatkin, I said I wanted a clause that ensured that I continued to have a single room at our hotels during away matches. Mike thought I was mad, but I had not shared for eight years and while the prospect of returning to the ranks appealed to me in many ways, as the only regular smoker in the side, I wanted my own space to pollute.

I got my way – not in writing, but with a verbal yes. I have packed in smoking during my career almost as many times as I have had innings: I picked the habit up again on one occasion after facing a torrid spell from Allan Donald just before the lunch break against Derbyshire. As I was sitting in the dressing-room, still with my pads on, Steve Barwick offered me a cigarette to help me calm down. It worked and I was hooked again. I will finally pack in when I retire from playing. Then there will be no Allan Donalds to set me off again.

20. OLLIE

Smoking and drinking: not virtuous habits for a professional sportsman. It is a question of balance and my fear for modern sport, not just cricket, is that by drawing up long lists of dos and don'ts all you do is ensure that players resemble each other. Isn't variety meant to be the spice of life? Nobody knows my own capacity better than I do, and it should be all about staying within your own boundaries, not ones laid down for you.

Image is everything, these days. I have been in a pub the night before a match, clutching a pint of sometimes shandy and at other times beer, and supporters have come up and had a go at me, saying I should be at home relaxing and have an early night rather than knocking one or two back. Relax is the word and that is what I like to do. The problem is not so much being seen in a bar as being seen to drink alcohol.

If I was standing around drinking a pint of orange-coloured liquid, I would not attract many comments: the assumption would be that it was orange juice and lemonade, rather than an alcopop. A number of rugby players have told me that when they go out they usually drink alcopops just to stop fans having a go at them. If you drank alcohol-free lager, you'd be deemed to be indulging rather than abstaining: it is a question of perception and while no player with any ambition to develop his career would be seen in a falling-down state in public either before or during a big match, there is nothing wrong with having a quiet couple to unwind.

Unfortunately, young players coming into the game are encouraged to stick to a narrower path in the belief that self-discipline will make them better players. The same applies on the coaching front, with risk-taking discouraged. I have never been one for uniformity, because players should be treated individually. The good man-manager recognises their distinctive qualities.

I went to a coaching seminar once with the former England off-break bowler Eddie Hemmings and one coach asked how he could turn youngsters who wanted to bowl fast into spinners. My response was that he was looking at the issue the wrong way round. Kids should be encouraged to bowl fast and slow and see which they prefer and which they are more adept at. They should also be allowed to bat everywhere in the batting order and given a go behind the stumps. Youngsters are going to want to bowl as fast as they can and bat high up the order, so it is a case of letting them find their level in their own time, giving an equal chance to all. Place the emphasis on enjoyment initially and do not worry about technique.

Cricket is seen as not the most arduous of occupations. It was once likened in athletic terms to brisk walking: a gross distortion of what the sport is all about! A season is mentally and physically gruelling and every time September comes around, now, I am ready to drop. It's not just the playing and the training – not forgetting the hours spent with the committee – but the travelling, the staying in hotels away from your family, the waiting for the rain to clear up and the inevitable occasional lean spell that you are afflicted with.

It can sound like a holiday, but there is a brutal side to cricket. Facing the likes of Allan Donald or Courtney Walsh is nobody's idea of fun. You have a split second to react and you know that precious few deliveries are going to be pitched up to you. Soccer and rugby matches are over in less than two hours; when the West Indians were at their best, without a medium-pace bowler let alone a spinner to relieve the diet of pace, there was no let-up from the barrage. To survive, let alone flourish, demands total concentration as well as skill and judgement. A few beers to unwind after all that mental effort is of far more therapeutic value, to me, than warming down, sipping some water and going home to think about the following day's play.

The game has changed more during my 16 years as a professional than in the previous 32. Many of the reforms have been beneficial: four-day cricket, coloured clothing, floodlit matches, points for a draw and the third umpire. There have been panic measures at times, with the authorities often jerking their knees after another series lost by England, but in general terms cricket has kept in touch with the times and the fact that it is the second most popular team sport in England after association football tells its own story.

All counties now pay attention to fitness, whereas 20 years ago players would casually make their way to the ground for a match. When Duncan Fletcher took over as the coach of Glamorgan in 1997, he introduced a fines system. If anyone was 30 seconds late for a training session, or the time laid down to turn up at the ground where we were playing, he would have to hand over £5. A second offence would earn a £10 fine, but if it happened a third time Fletch would throw the book at the miscreant. (All the money collected from the fines was donated to a charity which trained guide dogs for the blind.) Using mobile phones during match hours and sleeping in the dressing-room were also forbidden by Fletch, another sign of how the individual freedoms of old had become sacrifices to the team ethic. I myself banned smoking in the dressing-room, even though I was one of the few affected, because it was a case of thinking about the greater good.

The team comes first. That has always been my attitude. But when it comes to the way someone plays the game, you have to tread carefully. I have been very concerned about England A tours because I have seen too many players come back confused: they have had their actions and techniques questioned, not because of any major flaws (if there had been any, they would not have been on the trip in the first place) but because someone wanted them to bowl flatter or hold their bat straighter. You do not need that level of coaching on an England A trip and the Glamorgan slow left-arm spinner Dean Cosker, for one, is someone who suffered from the experience.

I have been criticised many times for playing a shot which looked loose and giving my wicket away too cheaply, but you play it as you see it. Any team needs balance. When Glamorgan won the championship in 1997 we had: Hugh Morris, someone who could bat all day without worrying how quickly he was scoring; Steve James, quick between the wickets and an acquisitive run getter; Adrian Dale, a batsman who could play it as the conditions demanded, quick or slow; myself, someone who always looked to play strokes; and Tony Cottey, obdurate and superb in a crisis. It was a top five of completely different but complementary players. There were occasions when Hugh Morris played like me. In 1996, during a Benson & Hedges Cup match against Kent in Canterbury, Hugh scored 136 not out as we reached our target of 209 with more than 17 overs to spare: he had reached his century off just 68 balls and he was facing an experienced attack. In order to qualify for the quarter-finals, we had to score the runs in 38.4 overs and Hugh set about the bowling immediately.

Similarly, there have been times when I have batted defensively and cautiously, curbing my attacking inclinations and playing for the team. But my general rule is that you serve the team best if you are true to yourself. There have been any number of times when I have been out to a bad ball, trying to cash in after being bowled a long-hop or a half-volley. I'm vulnerable to that sort of delivery after a lunch or tea break or at the start of a day's play, especially in Cardiff where the wicket tends to be slower than the nets in which we warm up. A typical dismissal happened in our championship match against Northamptonshire in Cardiff in 2000. We had been 39 for 2 overnight, after bowling them out for 229, and the first ball of the second morning that I received was the longest of long-hops, which I looked to pull mid-wicket for four. My timing was out and I offered an easy catch to mid-wicket. If I had a century for every time I'd been out in similar fashion, I would have overtaken Jack Hobbs, but your guiding principle must be to do what comes naturally.

Many of the Glamorgan records I hold are associated with quick scoring: the quickest century in a one-day match for the county; the fastest fifty in first-class cricket; the most runs taken off an over. There is no feeling like taking a side's attack apart to the point where their captain has no idea what to do. While there are some days when you wonder where your next run is going to come from, there are others when you can indulge yourself completely and get away with the outrageous. It is all about seizing the moment.

While I did not have any particular ambition to be a professional sportsman when I was a boy, I have done well out of cricket. The sport may lack the money and status of British soccer, but I think it is in better shape. It isn't overwhelmingly reliant on television for its income – not to the point where if the television bubble burst salaries would fall fast and a raft of players would be out of work. Nor are counties overloaded with players unqualified to play for England or any of the other home nations.

County cricket got a bad name because of England and, as I have argued, England's problems were more managerial than structural. If Duncan Fletcher, rather than Keith Fletcher, had been in charge of the 1994 tour to the Caribbean, the idea of splitting the championship into two divisions would never have got off the ground, because the national side would not have subsequently slumped to the bottom of the world rankings.

It's strange. When England do badly in soccer, which seems to be every time there is a major event, it is the manager who is held responsible and his job depends on success. When England did badly in cricket, which at one stage was virtually whenever they had a series, it was not the coach or manager who was deemed to be at fault but the structure. Perhaps it is 'not cricket' to point the finger at individuals, but blaming the county game for England's failure against West Indies in 1994, or against Australia in 1993, was looking for the easy way out. There was never any accountability and it showed.

I have no regrets about choosing cricket as a career or about anything I have done on the field. I could have achieved more, but all players can say that. I was at a dinner when someone said to me that I had been born too late, that I would have been a natural in the Compton era when the runs flowed along with the beer, when cavalier play was seen to be the stuff of national heroes. It is a rosy-eyed view of the past: uncovered wickets, a hectic schedule which meant you were either travelling or playing, and kit which makes you wonder how fast bowlers did not cause more injuries.

I believe that everyone is a product of their age and players are better off today than they ever have been before – not just in financial terms. Cars used to be a perk for capped players: now they are used as a bargaining counter by youngsters. In my early years with Glamorgan, I drove an old Opel and, coming back from Ebbw Vale one day, the clutch stuck. I was giving the wicket-keeper Terry Davies a lift back to Cardiff and every time I came to a roundabout I had to keep the car at full revs. Terry was whiter than any sheet by the time we made it back.

Talking to the captains of other counties in recent years, I reckon there's a sense that many young players feel they have arrived before they've even found the door – that they make demands before proving themselves. Some counties have given in and will pay the consequences in the future. Glamorgan have taken a tougher line, and I suspect we are the only county to have been asked a certain car question by a player. David Harrison, a promising all-rounder who made his first-class début in 1999, made an enquiry about a car which had everyone in stitches. He wanted to know if it was possible – and if the answer was yes, would the club be prepared to pick up the bill? – to add a fifth gear to his car, a 1.1 Fiesta.

That's another thing about cricket: you cannot invent some of the situations I have laughed at over the years. They say that the characters are dying out, and the push for conformity will accelerate that process, but I guess they will be saying the same in 50 years.

Not that I think the game was better when I started with Glamorgan in 1985. I would rather be beginning my career now. One concern I did have then was the amount of travelling we had to do. There were days when you would finish a game at 6 p.m., have a hurried shower and dash into your car to speed to the other side of the country for a match which started the following morning. Small wonder that it became common to be driving with nine points on your licence after being caught speeding. But for the sympathy of some policemen, I would have been banned at least twice. In August 1988, we played seven matches in the championship and four in the Sunday League: 25 days of cricket. We went from Eastbourne to Swansea to Abergavenny to Colchester to Wellingborough to Neath to Birmingham. We went in cars, rather than on a coach, because players lived all over the county and there would not have been a convenient pick-up point.

At the start of that season Rodney Ontong had been offered a Honda as his sponsored car. He refused it and said he wanted a Saab because, in his view, they were the safest vehicles around. If he was going to be involved in a crash, he wanted to maximise his chance of getting out of any wreck alive. As it turned out, the fact that he stuck to his guns and forced the county to back down saved his life.

Rodney was in his car with Steve Barwick. We had just drawn a match at Essex in unusual fashion: the scores were level when Derek

Pringle was run out off the last ball of the match. We claimed a tie, because Geoff Miller had been unable to bat and therefore, with nine wickets down, Essex were technically all out. There was a lot of confusion and the umpires eventually ruled that the match was a draw, a decision later confirmed by Lord's. The upshot was that we were late getting away from the ground and we were playing Northampton at Wellingborough School the following day. Rodney and Baz were involved in a horrible crash when a van pulled out in front of them suddenly. The police said they were both lucky to be alive and that if the car had not been a Saab they would probably not have made it. They'd have had little chance in a Honda.

The crash ended Rodney's career. He suffered a serious knee injury and only played five matches the following season before having to retire. He had yet to turn 34 and still had a lot of cricket left in him. Baz only picked up a stiff shoulder and sore neck and he was playing the following week at Llanelli in a Sunday League game; but, while fielding deep, he fell over a chair after discovering too late that he had no chance of catching a ball that was going for six – his back went and he missed the rest of the season.

Now that championship matches are all played over four days, the travelling is much easier because it is rare now that you have to dash from a match one night to another the next day. It does happen, though: when we played Surrey in the 2000 Benson & Hedges Cup semi-final, they had to travel to Cardiff from Canterbury and they hired a coach. It was not the most reliable of vehicles and they got into Cardiff late. When they made the trip back to London, after losing to us, it broke down on the M4 and an unhappy squad got home long after midnight.

My form of transport has come a long way since the days of my Avenger in New Zealand and Cortina in north Wales. I have had a Daimler for a few years, now, and it has a personalised number plate which is based on the nickname given to me by Tony Cottey back in 1992. Even though I had been at the club for seven years, the best anyone could dream up for me was 'Matt', before Cotts decided to call me 'Ollie' – after Oliver Reed (not Oliver Hardy!). This was based on my ability to enjoy a celebration and keep it going. I have had to slow down as I have got older, though. Despite never suffering from hangovers, I do feel tired now if I have too much the night before. There is no way I could do today what I did in 1989 and make a big century after having had one too many the previous evening.

No one has had to tell me to slow down: I know my own limits better than anyone and I do not consider relaxing with a beer the night before a match unprofessional. Each to his own, but only up to the point where behaviour off the field affects the team performance. Individuals matter more than ever, but the team comes first.

21. DECLARATION

The three-year contract I signed with Glamorgan at the end of the 2000 season will be my last as a player. It will take me through to the age of 38 and I suspect that my body will be telling me then to call it a day. I picked up a couple of injuries in 1998 and 1999, which were hard to shake off, and with more emphasis than ever before being placed on fitness, it is becoming a younger man's game.

Most counties used to have at least one player on their books who was in his 40s, often a slow bowler but sometimes a batsman. Alan Jones was 44 when he played his final season for Glamorgan in 1983, still good enough to make 1,000 runs for the summer. Fielding has become a key feature of the game today, and not just in one-day cricket. There is no room for passengers, nowhere to hide anyone and, as a consequence, the average age of sides is coming down.

I cannot see myself becoming an umpire, though you should never say never. They are coming under more and more pressure and the nature of the county game now – with promotion and relegation in the championship and the Sunday League – means players will become more aggressive and try it on with raucous appealing. The England and Wales Cricket Board have sent an edict to captains telling them that it is their responsibility to keep control of their players, which is fair enough up to a point. If you raise the stakes, as the board have done with structural changes which place a greater emphasis on success, you cannot expect patterns of behaviour to remain the same. I have been impressed with the England captain, Nasser Hussain, who received some shocking umpiring decisions while batting in 2000, but never lost his temper or composure and walked off with head held high. He set the right example and that is important.

Cricket has always been a hard sport, but today it is more mentally and physically demanding than it has ever been. In the coming seasons, I cannot see counties sticking together as they have done in the past: promotion and relegation means they are working against each other. There has been no transfer market in cricket and no challenge to the European Union, unlike soccer, to the rule which states that a county may only sign three List One players in a five-year period and no more than two in 12 months. A List One player is someone a county does not want to lose and it does not matter if he is uncapped or has hardly played any first-class matches. It is clearly a restrictive practice. Mark Ramprakash was talking about leaving Middlesex at the end of the 2000 season and there were no shortage of takers. He eventually joined Surrey. Now that the leading cricketers are contracted centrally by England, someone like Ramprakash, on the fringes of the national squad but likely to be available for the whole summer, is a better investment than Nasser Hussain or Darren Gough because these players may only play in a quarter of a county's championship matches.

Ramprakash had just had a Benefit at Middlesex, but the county's decline prompted him to think of moving elsewhere. With a year left on his contract, he was in a position where he could only go if Middlesex agreed to release him. With no transfer fees paid for cricketers, what incentive was there for the county to release its best player? I cannot see the transfer system surviving, even if it means a county threatening to take legal action. It has lasted until now because it has been based on consent, but that will not last.

Middlesex's dilemma over Ramprakash was accentuated by the loss of their bowler Richard Johnson to Somerset on a five-year contract. It was an excellent signing by Somerset, who knew that Andy Caddick will not play many championship matches for them while he remains in the England side. Johnson is not so much a stand-in for Caddick as a replacement and he is not that far away from the England squad.

In my five years as Glamorgan captain, we only signed one List One player: Alex Wharf. We were afraid of using up our quota in case someone we fancied signing became available. A player who feels he has been unfairly listed may appeal to the board, but the whole system is becoming anachronistic as counties look to put together increasingly attractive packages for players.

One of my fears about a two-division championship is that it could end up driving some counties to the point of bankruptcy. All counties depend on Test match receipts to make the difference between profit and loss, but the equal share-out which has always existed will start to be questioned: why should a side at the bottom of the second division receive the same as teams at the top of the first? The answer, 'Because they always have done', will become less and less acceptable.

A big surprise has been Middlesex's decline. As one of the Test match ground counties, they were expected to thrive and prosper in the new championship, but they are in danger of losing their base at Lord's and in fact played a number of matches in the 2000 season at Southgate in north London – a far less salubrious setting. I am confident that Glamorgan will always have a future because we are in effect a country, not just a county. If we ever lost our place in the championship, we could always apply to the International Cricket Council to be allowed to enter the World Cup as Wales and, perhaps, seek Test match status!

We are fortunate as a county that we have long had an excellent development programme where youngsters in Wales, the south especially, are quickly identified and fast-tracked. Our teenage wicket-keeper, Mark Wallace, is one to watch: other counties were chasing him before he signed a contract with us. The successful counties will be the ones that breed their own players, because there will be only so much money to throw at established players in other sides.

After the upheaval of the last five years, the county game needs some stability. The Benson & Hedges Cup was brought back after being dropped in its original format and resurrected as a Super Cup for one year. I would like to see it finally consigned to the history books, even though it earned us a long-awaited trip to Lord's in 2000. The group games were played from the middle of April, when the weather was always going to be a factor, and it appeared to be a competition run for the sake of it, thus becoming devalued.

I think the championship, the one-day league and one knock-out competition is enough. Getting rid of the Benson & Hedges Cup would open up a window which I would like to see partly filled by a regional tournament played over three weeks in May and used as a trial for that summer's forthcoming Test series. Three teams would play each other in four-day matches: this would be a step up from the championship and give the selectors a chance to see, in a competitive environment, players who are just below the national squad.

At the same time, I would operate a short-form game for the counties: 25 overs a side, with a limit on bowlers' run-ups and more attacking field regulations than the other one-day competitions to ensure more runs and boundaries. It would give counties the opportunity to look at youth and club players and it would also be a quick, explosive game which could be a way of attracting young spectators, especially if matches started at 4 p.m. when schools were out.

With the decline of cricket in schools, the sport has had to work hard to sell itself to youngsters in the past 20 years. The Cricket Board of Wales, set up three years, ago, have made enormous strides; but what youngsters need are role models, a reason why the likes of Waqar Younis and Jacques Kallis were such important recruits for us. The fact that England have started winning again will also help, and the 1–0 victory over Pakistan at the end of 2000 showed how far, and how quickly, the side has progressed under Duncan Fletcher.

There were times in that series when England were under pressure but, whereas before they may have played for themselves, players put the team first and the result was a victory against all the odds in the final Test. Fletch would be the first to admit that there is a long way to go, but without doubt he has helped make England more competitive again. They do not know when they are beaten and keep on fighting – and it's out of the players of today that the heroes of tomorrow are born.

As a lad I was hooked by the beauty of David Gower at the crease and the raw courage of Ian Botham, for whom no cause was ever a lost one. When Glamorgan won the championship in 1997, some of the players had development jobs in schools that winter and they were surprised to see how their profiles had risen because of their achievement. Nothing succeeds like success.

There are few ambitions that I have left to fulfil. The century for

England that I yearned for so long to score will never come. Time has left me behind, but at least I was given the chance. Perhaps if I had recorded a not out in Jamaica in 1994 rather than perishing for the cause, I would have kept my place in the England side for a while longer, but my lease was always going to be a short one. I was not made for England then. There is nothing to be gained by looking back and wondering about what might have happened. The past is history and all that matters is the future.

I will miss not facing Courtney Walsh again. He was the best bowler I have come up against in my career, an exceptional player whose performances were consistently high, whether he was playing for West Indies or Gloucestershire. He never gave you anything and he not only bowled at pace but also moved the ball in both directions. There was never any respite with him and, as he got older and his speed dropped slightly, he made up for it with some clever improvisation (such as a slower ball which made mugs of a number of world-class batsman). He has been a great cricketer and a smashing guy who, without any question, is one of the best overseas signings in the history of the county game. He would open the bowling in my Dream XI every time, along with another fast bowler who gave his all in the championship, Allan Donald.

Of the English bowlers I have faced, Neil Foster was probably the hardest to master. Injuries disrupted his England career, but you could never feel relaxed at the crease when he was bowling. He made you play at virtually every delivery and, like Walsh, combined pace with movement. He thought about his bowling rather than letting rip as fast as he could. Andy Caddick is also right up there: when I made my century at Taunton in the match which won us the 1997 championship, I took a few boundaries off him and that made the achievement all the more special because I'd always found him a handful. Ian Botham was capable of anything, even in the twilight of his career, and Graham Dilley was another quick bowler for whom I had the highest respect.

Shane Warne stands out among the spinners and, again, he showed the effect which success can have on youngsters. After he had burst onto the Test scene to help revive the dying art of leg-spin, kids suddenly started trying to be the next Shane Warne rather than another pace bowler. When Tony Lewis was the chairman of Glamorgan at the end of the 1980s, he made an attempt to sign the Pakistan leg-spinner Abdul Qadir, who had just established himself on the Test scene. Tony wrote him a letter and five years later received a reply from Qadir who said he would be delighted to join us. Another class bowler, Saqlain Mushtaq, is unusual, being an off-spinner with a wrong-'un; and I have always rated leg-spinner Ian Salisbury – I still cannot pick his googly.

We need to see a revival of spin bowling in the championship and, as I have argued before, that means better wickets. The England and Wales Cricket Board should have acted more decisively last year, when 20 wickets falling in a day was not the exception that it should have been. You can only take blaming a decline in batting standards so far; and while it can be argued that one-day cricket has seen batsmen lose patience too quickly, another factor in loose shots is the fear of being undone playing a defensive shot by a ball which does something unpredictable. Where there is doubt, there is not always discretion.

I sat for two years as the representative of the county captains on the board's cricket advisory committee. The committee was a mixture of administrators, coaches and players whose brief was to look at ways of improving the game on the field. I consistently argued for bowlers to be allowed one bouncer an over in one-day matches: they were already handicapped by only being allowed to bowl a certain number of overs, by field restrictions and by the rigid interpretation by umpires of what constituted a wide. A bouncer is a legitimate delivery and should be part of limited-overs cricket.

The advisory committee made a number of positive recommendations and it is one of the many things I shall miss, now that I'm no longer the Glamorgan captain. However, there are other aspects I am glad to have escaped from and five years is long enough. My son, Tom, has the makings of a very good cricketer and I want to help him as my father guided me, not by pushing and putting pressure on him, but by watching and being there for him as often as I can. He has to enjoy the game and realise that he is one of eleven.

Cricket is a great game. The late radio commentator Brian Johnston once said of his career, 'It has been a lot of fun.' That could serve as my epitaph. It was when driving from Canterbury in Cardiff in 1984, rejected by Kent, that I realised for the first time how much I wanted to be a professional cricketer. Not because I wasn't cut out to be anything else, but because a cricket field was where I could best express myself. It is for others to say whether I have been a success or a failure, but I have done it my way. Glamorgan may not be the most fashionable of counties, but there have been precious few cricketers who have come to us from England or abroad and not found themselves at home. Viv Richards used to revel in the atmosphere and appreciated the fact that he could enjoy his privacy off the field.

The challenge for all counties now is to avoid relying on Test matches for their income and to generate enough to pay the wage bills. That means not only being successful but also promoting themselves – not easy when cricket is only played domestically for less than half the year. It is a sport like any other, a team game made up of individual contests. As a batsman, you are on your own with a split second to make up your mind; and as word about you gets round the circuit, perceived weaknesses are ruthlessly exploited. Standing at the crease at a packed Test ground waiting for Walsh or Donald to bowl is not something for the faint of heart. Truly, the idea that cricket is a soft option is preposterous.

I've collected few mementoes of my career; I shall probably regret that in the years to come. I do have the bat I scored my maiden first-class century with. I also have the one I used at Taunton when we won the championship in 1997, the best piece of willow I ever had. I also got Michael Holding to sign a montage of photographs from 1988 when my helmet hit my wicket in the Benson & Hedges Cup semi-final, but I have never been one for sentiment.

Perhaps in future years I will take up coaching, but when my career as a player ends I will take a break from the game. It was sad to see Mike Gatting sacked as Middlesex coach at the end of the 2000 season. He had given so much to the club as a player, but perhaps needed to walk away for a few years before taking the coaching reins. Your relationship with the players changes when you switch from team-mate to coach and it is difficult to crack the disciplinary whip with guys you are used to cracking open cans with.

It is hard to select one out of all the innings I have played. My century against Yorkshire in 1985 was special because it was my first. When I made 160 against Somerset at Weston-super-Mare in 1987 their New Zealand batsman Martin Crowe, who was to go on and hit a century himself, said it was one of the best innings he had ever seen – that compliment meant a lot to me and I learned then the value of praise. Taunton in 1997 was memorable, as was Lord's in 2000: to score a century in a final proved that I did have the temperament to succeed on the big occasion.

And I once took the wicket of Marcus Trescothick, something to boast about now that he has established himself in the England side. In September 1999 we played back-to-back National League games against Somerset. The first was in Taunton, where Trescothick had earlier hit 167 to win the championship fixture against us in a match where most of the other batsmen struggled. The second was in Cardiff.

Duncan Fletcher was the Glamorgan coach then and he noted Trescothick's name after watching him hit his century. In the first National League game, I stumped him for a duck off Robert Croft. Adrian Shaw had been taken ill and I took over behind the stumps, not for the first or last time in my career. In the return game at Cardiff I had a problem when one of our seam bowlers, Andrew Davies, dislocated his shoulder after bowling just one over. With Adrian Dale struggling with back spasms and Kallis not fit enough to bowl all his nine overs, I needed someone to fill in.

I'd never taken a wicket in limited-overs cricket when I deceived Trescothick with my slower long-hop: he holed out to Alun Evans at mid-wicket, having had the choice of anywhere in the ground to smash the ball to. It was an important wicket, because he'd only made seven and we went on to win by 13 runs. It is my one and only wicket in one-day cricket and I cherish it.

It has been a lot of fun and it is still not time to declare. There are still a few more attacks to mount, a few more centuries to score, a few more catches to take and a few more beers to drink in celebration.

MATTHEW MAYNARD'S STATISTICS
by Andrew Hignell

CAREER BATTING RECORD FOR GLAMORGAN

M	I	N.O.	R	Ave	50	100	Ct/St
FIRST-CLASS CRICKET							
310	491	53	18,862	43.06	106	42	292/5
SUNDAY/NAT. LEAGUE							
211	203	16	5,941	31.7	39	4	88/2
BENSON & HEDGES							
54	54	6	2,121	44.19	–	6	17
NATWEST TROPHY							
42	40	3	1,559	42.14	12	2	20
IN ALL ONE-DAY GAMES							
339	327	29	10,747	36.06	69	13	139/2

CAREER BATTING RECORD IN
FIRST-CLASS CRICKET FOR OTHER TEAMS

M	I	N.O.	R	Ave	50	100	Ct/St
IN TESTS FOR ENGLAND							
4	8	0	87	10.87	–	–	3
FOR NORTHERN DISTRICTS							
19	27	1	1,485	57.12	7	5	19/2
FOR OTAGO							
8	13	1	333	27.75	1	–	7

CAREER BATTING RECORD IN LIMITED-OVERS CRICKET FOR OTHER TEAMS

M	I	N.O.	R	Ave	50	100	Ct/St
IN ONE-DAY INTERNATIONALS FOR ENGLAND							
12	12	1	156	14.18	–	–	4
FOR NORTHERN DISTRICTS							
11	11	2	395	43.89	–	1	6
FOR OTAGO							
20	20	3	654	38.47	4	1	10

CAREER BOWLING RECORD FOR GLAMORGAN

O	M	R	W	Ave
FIRST-CLASS CRICKET				
155.1	24	763	6	127.17
SUNDAY/NAT. LEAGUE				
10.4	0	64	1	64.00
BENSON & HEDGES				
5	0	38	0	–
NATWEST TROPHY				
3	0	8	0	–

CAREER-BEST PERFORMANCES FOR GLAMORGAN

First-class cricket	243	v Hampshire	So'ton, 1991
	3/21	v Oxford Uni	Oxford, 1987
Sunday/Nat. League	132	v Surrey	The Oval, 1997
	1/13	v Somerset	Cardiff, 1999
Benson & Hedges	151*	v Middlesex	Lord's, 1996
NatWest Trophy	151*	v Durham	Darlington, 1991

*denotes not out

CENTURIES FOR GLAMORGAN

v Derbyshire (4): 119 (Cardiff, 1987); 176 (Chesterfield, 1992); 145 (Derby, 1993); 118 (Cardiff, 1994)

v Durham (1): 134* (Cardiff, 1997)

v Essex (2): 122 (Chelmsford, 1996); 102 (Southend, 2000)

v Gloucestershire (7): 126 (Bristol, 1988); 191* (Cardiff, 1989); 129 (Cheltenham, 1991); 126 (Cheltenham, 1991); 164 (Abergavenny, 1995); 145* (Bristol, 1996); 119* (Cardiff, 2000)

v Hampshire (1): 243 (Southampton, 1991)

v Kent (2): 113* (Swansea, 1992); 170 (Canterbury, 1999)

v Lancashire (2): 138 (Old Trafford, 1995); 214 (Cardiff, 1996)

v Leicestershire (1): 103 (Leicester, 1995)

v Northamptonshire (1): 125* (Northampton, 1990)

v Nottinghamshire (2): 115 (Worksop, 1990); 204 (Cardiff, 1991)

v Somerset (4): 160 (Weston-super-Mare, 1987); 122 (Cardiff, 1988); 133* (Taunton, 1991); 142 (Taunton, 1997)

v Surrey (1): 103* (The Oval, 1991)

v Sussex (2): 127 (Cardiff, 1991); 112 (Hove, 1996)

v Warwickshire (1): 129 (Edgbaston, 1986)

v Worcestershire (2): 108* (Abergavenny, 1988); 161* (Worcester, 1997)

v Yorkshire (3): 102 (Swansea, 1985); 136 (Cardiff, 1996); 186 (Headingley, 1999) v South Africans (1): 101 (Pontypridd, 1994)

v Australians (1): 132 (Neath, 1993)

v Matabeleland (1): 101 (Bulawayo, 1995)

v Oxford University (2): 148 (Oxford, 1986); 110* (Oxford, 1993)

v Cambridge University (1) 100* (Cambridge, 1996)

*denotes not out

MAIN RECORDS HELD BY MATTHEW MAYNARD

IN FIRST-CLASS CRICKET

- Fourth-highest run scorer for the county, with 18,862. Only Alan Jones (34,056), Emrys Davies (26,102) and Gilbert Parkhouse (22,619) have scored more runs for Glamorgan.
- Scored a century on début for Glamorgan and also for Northern Districts.
- Youngest batsman to score 1,000 runs for Glamorgan, reaching the target in 1986 aged 20.
- Scored the fastest half-century for Glamorgan in the County Championship – in just 14 minutes against Yorkshire at Cardiff in 1987.
- Made a century against Somerset at Taunton in 1997 without any singles.
- Made the most runs in an over – 34 off Steve Marsh against Kent at Swansea in 1992.
- Took the fewest number of innings to reach 10,000 runs for Glamorgan – in just 276 innings.

IN LIMITED-OVERS CRICKET

- Most runs (10,747) in limited-overs cricket for Glamorgan.
- Only batsman in the UK ever to score centuries in both the semi-final and final of a major one-day competition – with 109 against Surrey at Cardiff and 104 against Gloucestershire at Lord's in the 2000 Benson & Hedges Cup.
- Fastest-ever century in one-day games for Glamorgan, with a

hundred in 58 balls against the British Universities at Cambridge in 1996.

- Most runs (2,121) for Glamorgan in the Benson & Hedges Cup and the highest-ever individual score in the competition, with 151 not out against Middlesex at Lord's in 1996.
- Most number of centuries in limited overs games – 13, held jointly with Hugh Morris.
- Most sixes in an innings in one day games – 7 against Surrey at The Oval in 1997.
- Shared highest-ever partnership for Glamorgan in one-day games, adding 259 for the third wicket with Hugh Morris against Durham at Darlington in 1991.